What Others are Saying...

"Patti Hathaway has a unique ability to tell stories and share the truth from the front-line employee perspective and those who are struggling with change. Her book is a must-read book for employees who want to move forward in corporate change. Untying the 'Nots' of Change is a quick read with lots of specific "how-to" techniques and insights."

Joyce Carter, Vice President of Human Resources, Fifth Third Bank, Western Ohio

"Patti Hathaway's original approach to managing change from an employee's perspective is refreshing. This book is for people who want to move beyond the challenges and pitfalls that change brings. Patti provides practical solutions that will enlighten the reader and encourage the discouraged."

James J. Buffer, Jr., Ed.D., Executive Director, The Collegiate Management Institute

"Change may be decided in the board room, but it is implemented by the rank and file. In her new book, Patti Hathaway addresses the very real fears and blocks that employees feel when business change is thrust upon them. Both front-line staff and leaders can benefit from Patti Hathaway's insight and and practical approach to change."

Earl R. Washburn, M.D., Administrative Physician, El Dorado Pediatric Medical Group, Inc.

"This is a wake-up call for employees who feel like they are losing the battle of their personal sanity to organizational change. This book provides a survival guide of practical and realistic tools to help employees move forward in change."

Janet C. Gibbs, Senior Vice President for Finance, Loyola University Chicago

"What a refreshing and entertaining approach to a serious subject! Change is inevitable and we all need to cope with it and plan for it as realistically as possible. This book will help you and your team make the necessary transition and have fun in the process."

George Morrisey, Author of 19 books, "Morrisey on Planning"

Untying the 'Nots' of Change (Before You're Fit to be Tied)
A Tool Kit of Personal Strategies for Change at Work
by Patti Hathaway, CSP
Editor: Tim Polk
Cartoonist: Clinton Cherry
Published by:
Destination Publications 1016 Woodglen Road Westerville, Ohio 43081-3236 U.S.A.

Printed in the United States of America
Library of Congress Cataloging-in-Publication Data Hathaway, Patti
Untying the 'Nots' of Change (Before You're Fit to Be Tied)
A Tool Kit of Personal Strategies for Change at Work / by Patti Hathaway
ISBN 0-9678731-0-X (pbk.)
Library of Congress Card Number: 00-190271

Untying the 'Nots' of Change

Before You're Fit to Be Tied

A Tool Kit of Personal Strategies
for Change at Work

Patti Hathaway, CSP

ACKNOWLEDGMENTS

To Juanell Teague, who sparked my uniqueness and helped me develop my initial thinking on change from an employee's perspective — thank you for helping me to be me!

Thanks to my husband, Jim Hathaway, and friend Brian Hanson for helping me come up with the terms for The Winner's Grid. I couldn't have done it without your expertise in sports terms. A heartfelt thanks to Jim for managing the business so I can do what I do best and for being my biggest fan and supporter.

A special acknowledgement to those who provided me with their technical assistance: Tim Polk, editor; Clinton Cherry, cartoonist; Gary Hoffman, typesetter and cover designer; Claudia Earlenbach, transcriptionist; Peggy Gallagher, research librarian; Jeanne Patton, proofreader; and Stephen Barnes, systems administrator.

Thanks to those of you who have reviewed and endorsed my book prior to its release: James J. Buffer, Jr., Ed.D., Joyce Carter, Colleen Dolgan, Janet C. Gibbs, George Morrisey, Earl R. Washburn, M.D., and Frank Wobst.

Most importantly, I would like to thank all the people who have attended my keynotes and seminars over the years and who have deepened my views on change. Many of your quotes and examples are included in my book. To the following people I want to extend my special thanks for allowing me to use their case studies and or quotes throughout my book: Mary Atkins, Muriel L. Ballou, Kathy Baugh, Sue Barrick, Keith Barsuhn, Matthew Beck, Dianne Biggs, Judy Bowman, Melissa Burwell, Jani Campbell, Joyce Carter, Maggi Channell, Jatana Davidson, Cindy DeWulf, Kevin M. Doherty, Susan English, Janet Gibbs, Shane L. Gilkey, Helen Green, Tom Griesdorn, Jacqueline D. Hymes, Margaret Klepic, Scott Owen Leonard, Laurel Lovely, William G. Martin, M.D., F.A.C.S, Ted A. McGuire, Beth Messer, Brian Morgan, Paul Pardi, Robert Pepper, Debi Robertson, Isaac A. Robinson, III, L.J. Roetzer, Cathy Ross, Rachel Snyder, William R. Stager, Debbie Swaine, Gloria J. Tucker, and Robert Zust. Thanks also to those people who allowed me to use their quotes but were fearful of having their name printed in this acknowledgement section.

Thanks to those authors whose books I read and quoted: Deloitte & Touche LLP and American Management Association study; Robert Enright, Ph.D.; Stephen Goldsmith; John MacArthur; Rick Maurer; the Mayo Health Letter; Price Pritchett and Ron Pound; Lewis Smedes; Manuel J. Smith; Dan Teitelbaum; and Alvin Toeffler.

Thanks to my e-mail newsletter subscribers, Matt Sherman and Frank D'Attomo, who sparked the book title idea.

TABLE OF CONTENTS

PART ONE

Why We Become "Fit to Be Tied"
When Our Organization Changes

Introduction: Are You Sitting Down?

Not all change is good, yet change is inevitable. Recognize that change surrounds you, it leaves no one untouched, and change is here to stay. Your ability to deal with rapid change will become your most important professional and personal development skill.

Chapter 1: Change Is a Many Splintered Thing

Understand the various phases you will experience as you go through the Cycle of Resistance. Identify the losses that create personal paralysis and keep you from moving forward in change.

Chapter 2: If You've Been a Cat All Day, You'll Be a Cat at Night

Evaluate your reaction to change and how it impacts you professionally and what your reaction to change is costing you personally.

PART TWO

Communication Strategies to Untie the
"Nots" in Organizational Change

Chapter 3: Shiver Me Timbers ...

Discover strategies you can use to deal with the upheaval caused by new leadership.

Chapter 4: The Thrill of Victory, The Agony of Criticism

Become coachable. Break through your resistance to change by channeling other people's criticism into productive results.

INTRODUCTION:
ARE YOU SITTING DOWN?

*"There are lots of unknowns with the proposed changes!
I feel alternatively excited and challenged, or exhausted and
stressed. How much more work can I do? When will I have
enough time to do things right and not just get things
done?"*

Social Worker

It was one of those phone calls that you fear. The voice on the line said, "Patti, are you sitting down?" Why do we automatically believe that what follows is going to be negative? My boss was on the other end of the phone. He explained that the public seminar company I was under contract with had been bought out by a British organization. The new company had decided to close our division. The phone call came just two months after I left my full-time training position in order to venture out on my own.

Two opposing signals went off in my mind as I hung up: opportunity and danger. My optimistic side thought that this would be a great opportunity to prove that I really could make it as a professional speaker without a monthly contract to fall back on. But the pessimistic side of me flashed a danger signal. Will we be able to pay our mortgage and car payments? Should I go back and beg for my old job, the one I had left two months ago?

The Chinese have a symbol that combines danger and opportunity. It is the symbol of "crisis." Today so many organizations and individuals are in crisis because of change. Organizations today are undergoing massive reorganizations, re-engineering, downsizing, mergers, acquisitions, software and hardware changes, new management....and the list goes on and on.

In a 1994 study of change by Deloitte & Touche LLP and the American Management Association, approximately 84% of American companies are undergoing at least one major business change as they respond to a rapidly evolving marketplace. In fact, nearly half (46%) of the respondents reported that they have at least three major change programs underway.

The workplace of the new millennium will be no different. This rapidly changing workplace demands a new level of adaptability on the part of workers. Old ways of doing things do not work in this changing marketplace. Those organizations that stand still will be overcome by their competition.

> *"I understand and know that the current changes are based on the evolution of the organization. It doesn't always make them easy — change is still stressful. I know that organizations that never change are not going to meet the needs of the consumer. However, some of the direction and changes have been made so quickly that it has been hard to get on with our work!"*
>
> *Pilot Project Coordinator*

People will either become one of two things in change: (1) they will look at change as danger and become a change victim, or (2) they will look at change as an opportunity and become a change agent. No one can straddle the fence thinking to themselves, "What am I going to be today?" You must become either a change agent or a change victim. The good news is this — the choice is yours!

An "agent" is someone who produces an effect; an instrument by which a guiding intelligence achieves a result. An agent is proactive and involved in the change. A victim is a person who is adversely affected by something or someone. They wait for an event to happen and then react to it.

The challenge we face in choosing between becoming a change agent or change victim reminds me of a philosophical child I saw in a cartoon. A little boy says to his buddy, "I thrive on change." The little buddy says to the boy, "You? You threw a fit this morning because your mom put less jelly on your toast than yesterday." To

You can become a change agent or a change victim — the choice is yours.

which the boy adamantly replies, "I thrive on making other people change."

Isn't that true for most of us? It's great if we're in charge of the change. But if we're not in charge, we're challenged. If I owned that British company, I'd be thinking this was a great decision to shut down the public seminar division. Unfortunately, I wasn't in charge of the change. Oftentimes we don't have a say in the changes at work. Will you respond as a victim or as a change agent?

> "*Some individuals (and I hope I'm not one of them!) seem to resist change and react negatively no matter what may be done to prepare them or involve them. However, for most people it seems their reactions vary greatly depending on how much control or input they feel they have in the situation.*"
>
> *Environmental Specialist*

Thirty years ago Alvin Toffler's book *Future Shock* opened with these words: "...between now (1970) and the twenty-first century, millions of ordinary, psychologically normal people will face an abrupt collision with the future. Citizens of the world's richest and most technologically advanced nations, many of them will find it increasingly painful to keep up with the incessant demand for change that characterizes our time. For them, the future will have arrived too soon."

Toffler's future is here, and it's more painful than most anticipated. We think change is great . . . until it affects my company, my department, my job, or me. We then act shocked and disturbed, as if we had no inkling organizational change would affect us so personally.

> 🉐 *"I believe our jobs will change substantially. In our 'old world' our approach to system development was very 'flat' in that we had one and only one customer to satisfy (the one asking for the change). Tomorrow's world will be much more 'round' in that every request will have to be evaluated from the standpoint of the whole company. This will take a brand new mind set. Employees believe that the new computer system is good, as long as it does not mean I have to change! The other 'popular' opinion is finally you're going to fix that other group . . . they have always been screwed up."*
>
> *Project Manager*

Your mission should be to become a change agent. First however, you need to understand the current reality of change within the work setting. Let's examine the private sector in corporate America. In their book, *The Employee Handbook for Organizational Change,* Price Pritchett and Ron Pound stated that the 1980's was the "decade of instability." Here are just some of the changes that occurred:

- Nearly half of all U.S. companies were restructured.
- More than 80,000 organizations were acquired or merged.
- Several hundred thousand companies were downsized.
- At least 700,000 organizations sought bankruptcy protection in order to continue operating.
- More than 450,000 organizations failed.

Those changes affected millions of people.

Flash forward to the 1990 scene of mergers and acquisitions: From the 1997 total of $655 billion to more than $1.75 trillion dollars spent in 1999 in the U.S.A. ($3.44 trillion worldwide), the worldwide merger frenzy continues to spiral upward. This is far beyond what experts had predicted in earlier years. As mergers keep increasing

> *In times of drastic change, it is the learners who inherit the future. The learned usually find themselves equipped to live in a world that no longer exists.*
>
> Eric Hoffer

every year, more and more people are affected by significant levels of organizational change. Add to the merger boom increasing competition, organizational reorganizations, massive technological advances, and changes in governmental programs and you will find a rare person NOT affected by change.

What about the public sector? Having worked extensively with both private and public sector organizations, I see a trend. What happens in the private sector happens in the public sector about 10 years later. Consider this: in corporate America during the 1990's there was an emphasis on increasing the competitive edge. This led to the drastic increase in mergers and acquisitions we see today. There was also considerable outsourcing. Did you realize that during the 1990's, General Motors was surpassed as the single largest private sector employer in the United States by Manpower Temporary Agency? Later, Manpower was acquired by Adecco, another staffing service company which in 1998 placed over 2.5 million temporary employees in 52 countries. That tells you a great deal about where we are headed.

With decreasing unemployment, companies are finding it harder to find and keep good employees. One of the results of this trend is that more and more private sector employers are paying for performance in order to keep their best employees.

How does this affect the public sector? These same trends have already begun and will continue to expand in the public sector in the year 2000 and beyond. There will be more competition. The result may be an increase in mergers and consolidations within the public sector. In the State of Ohio in early 1999, the Department of Human Services merged with the Bureau of Employment Services.

Since there were many overlapping services, it only made sense to consolidate the employment services areas. The reality is that people are beginning to say to their elected officials, "Hey, we have done this already in the private sector. It's time you do it. Prove to the voters that your services are efficient, don't overlap, and are designed with the public in mind. If not, I'll vote for someone who is willing to make changes that result in greater efficiencies and better service."

Privatization in government is comparable to the private sector's outsourcing. Here is an example in the public sector. The mayor of Indianapolis, Stephen Goldsmith, has written a book called *The 21st Century City, Resurrecting Urban America.* Goldsmith believes that just because government has a duty to ensure that citizens receive certain services, it doesn't mean the government must produce those services itself. He advocates that private companies can do a better job of delivering most services than government. And he's proven it. Goldsmith called for competitive proposals for managing the city's international airport. The company that won the competitive bid reduced the airport cost per passenger from $6.70 in 1994 to $3.87 in 1996. The company actually increased revenue from the concessions by fifty percent without overcharging patrons. The privatization movement has been very successful in some arenas and has had mixed reviews in others.

> Everyone thinks of changing the world, but no one thinks of changing himself.
>
> Leo Tolstoy

The question is — how do you react to change when it affects you directly? The purpose of this book is NOT to repeat the age-old mantra, change is good, because we all know that not all change is good. In fact, you will learn that most change is painful. The purpose of this book is to help you see how you can choose to become a change agent even if you are not in control of the change itself. The goal is to help you view change as an opportunity rather than a threat or a danger.

This book focuses on specific strategies which will help you move forward in change so that you will not become another victim of organizational change. In Chapter 1: *Change Is a Many Splintered Thing,* you will begin to understand the various phases you will experience as you go through the Cycle of Resistance to change. You will identify the losses that create personal paralysis and prevent you from moving forward when change occurs.

Chapter 2: *If You've Been a Cat All Day, You'll be a Cat at Night* will help you evaluate your reaction to change and how it impacts you professionally. You will also learn how your reaction to change may be costing you personally. In Chapter 3: *Shiver Me Timbers...* you will discover communication strategies you can use to deal with the upheaval caused by new leadership.

Learning how to become coachable during change will be covered in Chapter 4: *The Thrill of Victory, The Agony of Criticism.* You will learn how to break through your resistance to change by channeling other people's criticism into productive results.

> Almost anything you do will seem insignificant but it is very important that you do it . . . You must be the change you wish to see in the world.
> Mahatma Gandhi

The very powerful skill of forgiveness is taught in Chapter 5: *An Eye for an Eye and A Tooth for a Tooth Can Leave You Blind and Toothless.* This chapter will help you recognize that one key to healing your past is learning to forgive others who have wronged you. This allows you to move forward into your future.

Chapter 6 provides the critical skills of *Whining With Purpose.* You'll develop your ability to give critical feedback to others and provide input about organizational changes in a purposeful manner. Learning how to Gracefully Exit and let go of what you cannot control is taught in Chapter 7: *When You're at the End of Your Rope, Let Go!* We'll also strategize ways to streamline your job.

> *"I have never taken well to major changes in my life. I know that change is inevitable. I would like to understand the various change issues. I would like to discover tools to increase productivity and energy in times of change. I would also like to learn techniques to help me and others cope with change."*
> *Secretary*

Do you want to feel the power of a Championship Focus by taking action in the areas you can control and encouraging others to do the same? You won't want to skip Chapter 8: *Bye-Bye, Boo Bird,* where you are provided with the skills to help you feel powerful even when you are not in charge of the organizational change.

Chapter 9: *All Stressed-Out and No Place to Go* will help you build a plan to manage all the stress that accompanies organizational change. Continuing on the theme of self-management skills, read Chapter 10: *When the Going Gets Tough, the Tough Get Talking.* You will learn how to develop your positive attitude about change by utilizing the strategy of self-talk.

We conclude with an Action Plan: *It's Not Whether You Win or Lose, It's That You're Playing the Game* by helping you design a Personal Action Plan to move yourself forward in organizational change.

The quotes and examples you read throughout the book are from real people I have met in my programs or have served as my clients. The personal quotes list only a job title because most of these individuals still work for their organization. Names in the examples

> *Insanity is doing the same thing over and over again and expecting different results.*
> Einstein

are changed to protect the identities of those who were willing to share their lives via the examples with you. In the Acknowledgement Section their names are listed with my grateful appreciation. This book is about real situations and real answers, not just theory.

Change is now the norm, not the exception. You are probably reading this book because you are frustrated with organizational change, and you want practical suggestions for what to do about it. You have come to the right place. I hope you will read this book and learn skills that you will be able to use for a lifetime. When the British company closed down the training division where I was employed, I decided to pursue my dream of becoming a professional speaker. I've never regretted making that decision because my life changed so significantly — for the better! Are you ready to become a change agent? It will change your life, too!

PART I:

WHY WE BECOME 'FIT TO BE TIED' WHEN OUR ORGANIZATION CHANGES

CHANGE IS A MANY SPLINTERED THING

"Most people are concerned about whether or not their positions will be eliminated or changed drastically. Also, how will this impact my family? Are we changing for change's sake or is it in the best interest of those people we serve? Not all GOOD IDEAS work or are feasible!"

Job Developer

I was coming down with a cold. At first I tried to ignore the symptoms. The scratchy throat, the sneezing, the tiredness — they'll go away, I said to myself. I just can't afford to get sick right now. I'm too busy. I'll just pretend it's not happening. Half of getting sick is in your mind, right?

But then it happens. I get sick. Isn't it amazing how there is never a "good time" to be sick? I headed off to the pharmacy to stock up on cold medicines, cough drops, and anything else that would help reduce my pain and discomfort. Why is it that we don't really appreciate our health until we lose it?

What does fighting a cold have to do with organizational change? What we do when we're sick and what we do when we are forced to go through organizational change is very similar. We instinctively and automatically resist illness because it's not the health we are used to. We instinctively resist change because it's not what we're used to in our organization.

The Resistance Cycle depicts what typically happens to people in organizations that are going through change. In Phase 1: *Ignore the Pain* — we do just that — we ignore the fact that a change is

even occurring, just as I ignored that I was getting a cold. Our focus is on what others are doing to us. We make comments such as, "Why are they doing this to me?" or "It will never happen." We tend to avoid listening to or reading any information that pertains to the change(s). We feel overwhelmed when we're not in total denial.

> 🌀 *"The reaction has been mostly a "let's just wait and see" thing. Staff appear willing to be passive in their approach toward change, letting the change come to them versus running out to greet it. I anticipate a good amount of anxiety and resistance to a new way of doing things."*
>
> *Manager of Staffing*

It's almost as if we put on big sunglasses, but instead of seeing the change, we are really ignoring the fact that the change is occurring around us. To paraphrase an old saying — if we can see no change and hear no change, no change can happen to us! I saw a very funny cartoon recently where the boss says to his staff, "Companies must learn to embrace change." The staff members are simultaneously thinking, "Uh, oh. It's another management fad. Will it pass quickly or will it linger like the stench of a dead woodchuck under the porch?" The boss states, "I think we should do a change newsletter." The staff sigh and think to themselves, "Woodchuck."

We want to believe that the latest change really is a fad and will pass quickly. Sometimes it does. Many times, however, we will need to adjust to a new way of doing our job as a result of the change. When we *Ignore the Pain,* we are so focused on the past and what we're losing that we cannot even begin to see the potential future which is inviting us.

Ignore the Pain tends to be the shortest-lived phase in the **Cycle of Resistance** because, in most cases, organizational change is forced upon us with no input or choice of our own. However, you can only ignore change for so long until it's knocking at your door or it lands in your lap.

> When one door closes, another opens: but we often look so long and regretfully upon the closed door that we do not see the one which has opened for us.
> Alexander Graham Bell

When we begin to *Feel the Pain* in Phase 2, we recognize that this change is going to be more painful than initially thought. The focus shifts from an emphasis on others (and what THEY are doing to us) to a focus on self (how is this change going to affect ME?). We ask questions like: How will the changes affect my job? Will I still like what I do? Will they replace me with a computer?

With this self-focus, we experience a sense of loss over what used to be. We mourn the "good old days." Some people are overwhelmed and depressed, while others simply feel disconnected from the organization. We feel like we have no choice or control over decisions which are affecting us directly.

"I feel sadness. We've no identity. It's been lost for 7 years. Employee and Company loyalty is gone forever. The loss of individuals with whom I've worked for many years is a great loss. It's very emotional to lose individuals who have contributed so much."

Desktop Technician

I find the most interesting reactions to change in copy rooms and staff lunchrooms of organizations. That's where you find out how people are really feeling about the work changes. People post anonymous cartoons, posters, and poems. In one client's office I found a poster that totally epitomizes this phase. It's a drawing of a man pointing a pistol (like the Uncle Sam poster where Sam is pointing at you). The caption reads, "Go ahead and make one more change!"

Focus on Others

| Ignore the Pain | New Growth |

Yesterday TODAY **Game Plan for Tomorrow**

| Feel the Pain | Heal the Pain |

Focus on Self

In Phase 2, people are on the edge. They're in serious pain. For example, the organization announces something minor, such as everybody has to pay five dollars more per month on their health insurance plan. That's a pretty minor change. But there will be an outcry. People will be upset. It's not the five dollars a month, it's the fact that it is ONE MORE CHANGE! The pain is evident and very real despite the insignificance of the change. At times it seems like we are dragged kicking and screaming into a new change. Holding on to the past seems to cement some of us to the floor.

One thing we must realize is that some of us come to work to escape a painful personal situation. Coming to work for some of us is a vacation. When the organization announces a change, the work change in combination with our personal changes may be enough to push us over the edge. You need to realize it's not just the organizational change that is affecting us. Our pain may be related to the upheaval in our personal lives. The organizational change merely makes our life all that more difficult.

So, why do we feel the pain so deeply? The main reason is because we feel we have no control. Many of us have not been told exactly what will be changed, just to expect change. In fact, in the Deloitte Touche/AMA study, 47% of the executives admitted that their communication about change was not effective. Perhaps we could manage the change if we knew what we were managing. Uncertainty is the worst problem. Dictating change seems to be the responsibility of someone else. Others are going to make decisions which impact our lives. We have no input, no say. This leaves us

At times we are dragged kicking and screaming into a new change. Holding on to the past seems to cement some of us to the floor.

feeling hopeless and in pain. The depth of your pain will be a direct reaction to one or more of these concerns:

EVALUATING OUR SKILLS AND CONDITIONING

Perhaps you used to be a "franchise player" (a valued team member who gets paid well). Now you wonder if you have the skills to succeed in the new world of technology and the new ways of doing business. Isn't it hard to admit you don't know how to do something or that you may now lack the skills necessary to succeed? Perhaps you're asking yourself, "Has the game passed me by?"

"Some employees have been fearful that the changes will leave no place for them, that their knowledge and experience will not be utilized in the new emphasis as a result of internal barriers/labels (my work versus your work, rather than our work). As time passes, the internal barriers have not changed

and have become even more entrenched — the fears have not been assuaged."

Engineering Manager

A major change in the nature of your job may require retraining or learning new things. Most of us view those kinds of changes with anxiety.

I remember when some of my colleagues attempted to convince me to upgrade my software. I refused for a long time. I liked what I had. It was my friend. It was simple. I knew where to find things, and I felt competent. What if I couldn't find the information I needed on the new system? It would slow me down. I didn't have time to waste.

> **Stability does not always mean security, and security does not require stability**
> **Author Unknown**

I finally caved in. I upgraded. Were my fears realized? Some were. But many others were not. Today I love my new software, even though I don't understand it completely. Learning new technology is where the future is. If I'm going to succeed, I must be willing to learn and upgrade my skills along with the technology I use. It's not that we're afraid of technology. We're afraid we won't be successful in learning the new technology. Has the technology game passed you by?

"The main issue I'm worried about is how we unrealistically expect human productivity to parallel the geometric growth of technology. Given that we live in a country where the incidence of stress-induced disease is very high, we'll be seeing the effects of this very soon."

Accountant

Consider just some of the technology changes we've seen over the last ten years:

- Current cell telephone users are numbered at 90 million worldwide. The experts project cell telephone usage to pass the 330 million mark by 2002.

- The number of computers in the workplace has soared from 5 million to 75 million in the last ten years. In 1995, people bought more computers than television sets for their homes.

- Industry experts suggest that there are more than 110 million pagers in use around the world. Some European countries registered an increase in pager use in the last year by more than 45%.

- There was a 118% increase from 1997 to 1998 in the number of registered domain names on the Internet.

- More than 7.3 billion commercial e-mail messages are sent each day in the U.S.

- All of this is compounded by a recent study which indicates that employees send and receive an astounding 190 messages per day.

What is so difficult about technological changes is the fact that we often get new technology without evaluating or discarding the old processes that sometimes went with the old technology. So, we are left with trying to do our old job with tools that don't support us. Or, we do two jobs — the old one and a new one that came along with the new technology. In Chapter 8, we'll discover some questions which will help streamline jobs to avoid this tendency.

LACK OF JOB SECURITY

There is an uncertain feeling about the role we will play and whether or not we have job security. With one out of four employees being affected by a corporate merger or acquisition, we may ask questions like:

- Where do I fit in this organization?

- Do I have a job? What is it? Will my job be outsourced after the merger is completed?

- Will my responsibilities change? Will I be assigned a new manager (again!)? Will I have to relocate?

- Will training be scaled back as a result of the merger, or will we be given additional avenues for education?

Many of us have the tendency to worry more about protecting our turf and territory than contributing to the organization's success. Think about it . . . if there are two of you in your department and you believe only one job will remain due to a reorganization, what would

> Once we truly know that life is difficult — once we truly understand and accept it — then life is no longer difficult. Because once it is accepted, it no longer matters.
>
> M. Scott Peck

you do? Most of us would be going for the "Most Valuable Player" award. That is, our goal would be to show that we are more valuable than our co-worker in an attempt to save our job. If I'm making myself look indispensable, what do you think I'm going to make you look like? Dispensable. Where is team unity in this scenario? Nowhere. This is one of the clear dangers with organizational change.

Change is particularly difficult for some of the "veteran" employees in organizations today. They have become comfortable with their roles staying the same for years. They may have even been in the same building and office for years and years. We can fall into a rut when we don't change our path once in awhile. Someone once defined a "rut" as a grave with both ends dug out.

"How do you change the mindset of a 20+ year employee who harbors the reflection upon what the company offered a number of years ago when it was a much smaller company, operating in a lesser competitive environment, on a much smaller scale? That individual doesn't want to look toward the future, simply to relish the past; is not motivated to meet daily challenges . . . simply to retire in the ranks where s/he currently resides."
Vice President and General Manager

We may be concerned about a change in our perceived status if our position title is changed (even if our job has not been changed). One organization I know of is shifting from multiple job descriptions to one — "Do what it takes." How would you deal with such a significant philosophical shift? A critical question to consider is, "Am I more concerned with my own statistics or the team's success?" In Chapter 4 you will learn how to become more coachable in your position so that you will not fall prey to the "Most Valuable Player" syndrome.

LACK OF TEAMWORK

"The support that was once there has been stripped away. It feels like a break up of a family. We're working to rebuild but it will take some time to feel whole again."

Administrative Assistant

Aside from the "Most Valuable Player" syndrome already mentioned, several other things often occur with teamwork when organizations go through change. For example, if you are a new employee (like a rookie athlete), you may be overlooked because you lack a proven track record. Even though you probably bring a fresh, new perspective to the organization, it is often ignored. On the other hand, maybe you are a long-tenured employee who, like a veteran athlete, may worry because your skills may be diminishing and you are not recognized as the star you once were.

Somehow, somewhere is the mysterious "Plan," and you would feel so much better if they would just let you in on the secret "Plan."

You may worry if your position is combined and you are made into a "generalist" instead of being a "specialist." While you may be questioning why your work hours need to change, your colleagues from a different department might wonder why your department worked the same hours all these years. Often departments act as if they exist in their own silo — distinct and apart from the rest of the organization. Often these silos do not understand how they impact the other departments' tasks/projects and how this separateness ultimately affects the organization as a whole.

As players on a team, all of us want to feel significant, that we have value. Most of us want to know, *"How can I contribute value to my team?"* When we are going through change, our roles get blurred. We tend to protect our old roles and ways of doing things because that is all we know. There may not a clear understanding of what each person on the team is to do. Some roles overlap. Because of a lack of communication among team members we may not even be clear about who is responsible for what.

When our roles aren't clear, we find it difficult to be any part of a team. Thus, teamwork can easily disappear during organizational change, and things can become very chaotic.

> *"The changes are positive for our program. However, these are chaotic times. Communication is essential. We try but I think we are slipping into separate entities and that is exactly what we wanted to change. Is this project going to work? Will we continue this project even if it is not successful?"*
>
> *Habilitation Manager*

WHAT IS "THE GAME PLAN"?

We wonder — what's coming next and WHY? It sometimes seems like organizations change just to avoid becoming stagnant, with no idea of whether the change is "better" or not. Many people are left feeling devalued/worthless in the face of upcoming changes.

When change happens in an organization, we quickly begin questioning the direction and where the organization is going. This is particularly true in organizations undergoing a leadership change. Many new bosses are like a new coach: They don't ask for the players' input because they were hired to turn the team around.

Focus on Others

Ignore the Pain	New Growth

Yesterday TODAY **Game Plan for Tomorrow**

Feel the Pain	Heal the Pain

Focus on Self

We begin asking: So what is the game plan for tomorrow? Where are we headed? Is someone planning for our organization's success? Is anyone in charge here?

You probably believe that top management has "The Game Plan" figured out, they just aren't telling you. You recognize that they are asking for your input, but you see no evidence of them taking your input into consideration, right? Somehow, somewhere is the mysterious "Plan," and you would feel so much better if they would just let you in on the secret "Plan."

> *"There is sentiment that they (employees) feel we (managers) go away to meetings and secretly plot their fate and spring it on them. Among the veterans, it is difficult for them to see beyond the change — they're always wondering "What's next?" From a morale standpoint, I think the professional staff are wondering if more changes are coming around the corner and if it will involve them."*
>
> *Executive TV Producer*

The number one complaint I hear from employees is, "I just wish management would ask for my input." The number one complaint I get from managers is, "I just wish my employees would take more initiative to give us more input." You both want the same thing but don't appear willing to come halfway.

Here's the reality about the game plan. Most organizations are creating "The Plan" as they go along. There isn't one document that specifies the exact, detailed description about where your organization is headed and where you specifically fit into the plan. By nature, the game plan must be fluid in order for the organization to succeed in this fast-changing world.

I know you're thinking to yourself: You mean those guys are being paid the "big bucks" and they don't know where we are headed? We are in deep trouble. The reality is that they need your input whether they ask for it or not. See Chapter 6 for ways you can give feedback that will be accepted (or "whine with purpose" as I like to call it).

WILL WE MAKE THE PLAYOFFS?

🌀 *"I'm concerned about the vision and plan for the university. I lack confidence in our leadership. Does anyone know what they are doing? and why? It feels like a ship without a captain."*
Associate Director

Will your team/organization be successful? Even if your team or organization succeeds, will you be cut from the team and put on waivers? Do you feel like there is a lack of vision? Do you find it difficult to not know where you stand on the team or within your organization?

Perhaps you've asked yourself these questions as you've experienced organizational change. These are gut-wrenching questions to consider and are questions only your organization will eventually answer. What is important for you to understand is that you will FEEL the pain that change is causing you before you can begin the healing process.

On the other hand, if you ignore the pain and don't take the time to understand what causes it, you won't know what and how to begin the healing process. Remember the old adage, "No pain, no gain!" That is true for people experiencing organizational change as well — we must have pain before there is organizational gain.

In Phase 3: **Heal the Pain,** the focus is still on self and how the changes will affect me. But now we are (or should be) past "feeling" the pain. The focus on yesterday has turned to a look at tomorrow. It is important to note that we are still on the bottom of the cycle, and we are still dealing with pain.

"Have you ever waltzed? Both partners are moving; but, one is leading and the other is dancing backwards. I haven't been part of the lead group and sometimes it feels like we're moving in the wrong direction. I believe in the quote by Alvin Toffler: 'Change is not merely necessary to life. It is life.' I try to keep positive — but it can be difficult when you don't understand why some decisions are made."

LAN Administrator

One of the main things people experience in this "healing" phase is organizational chaos and indecisiveness. Committees or task forces are one form of indecisiveness. The organization isn't completely sure what the details of the game plan are, so they assign a committee to help them figure out how the plan should be implemented.

As a result of the anxiety that comes out of chaos, we just want our boss to tell us what "The Plan" is. In reality, there is no specific, concrete, well-defined, set-in-stone plan — particularly when it comes to defining the how-to's of the change that is being introduced. Most game plans are fluid in nature and may and will change as the needs dictate.

> There is a force that somehow pushes us to choose the more difficult path whereby we can transcend the mire and muck into which we are often born. Despite all that resists the process, we do become better human beings.
>
> M. Scott Peck

"Time is an issue. This "car" is being built as it's moving along. Lack of preparation kills momentum. Staff crave information and are frustrated due to the lack of information."

Vice President

It's similar to a coach at halftime giving the team information and revising the game plan prior to the second half. Sometimes the strategy/game plan the coach originally designed doesn't work out in the "real world." Effective team players need the strength and ability to give honest input from a front-line perspective. Why return to the game with a plan that you know will not work?

The second critical aspect of this phase is to learn to forgive those who have wronged you in the past so you can move into your future. Anger and bitterness toward our boss or a co-worker keep us stuck in the past. We are unable to focus on tomorrow if we keep re-living the situation where someone wronged us. This critical skill of forgiveness will be covered in depth in Chapter 5.

Eventually, people build enough trust in the leadership of their organization to consider committing themselves to Phase 4: **New Growth** for Tomorrow. It means making a commitment to a non-exact, perhaps even vague tomorrow. The best analogy for this final phase is marriage. For those of us who are married, how many of us really knew what marriage was going to be like before we got married? Very few of us. Yet most of us hopefully and willingly made a commitment to our spouse — even with all the unknowns. Does this mean that every single day we absolutely love and adore our spouse? Hardly.

I once heard a well-known evangelist interviewed about his fifty-plus years of marriage to his wife. He was asked the question if he and his wife ever discussed divorce. Without hesitation, he replied, "Divorce no, murder yes." I think I'm in good company and so are you. Even though we love our significant other, we may not absolutely *like* them all the time.

☞ *"Basically, the changes that have occurred I have tried to let slide off my back without reacting to it. After all, the change we're now experiencing is inevitable so I figure it's best to go with the flow rather than fight the current. I just hope things don't get lost in the shuffle. I really liked my old job, my benefits, etc. so I can only hope that this merger will produce similar benefits and a feeling of contentment."*

Software Manager

The same is true with your organization. When you make the commitment to **New Growth** for your organization and its vision for tomorrow, it doesn't mean you will always like what's going on in your organization or the direction it is headed. But, it also doesn't mean you are any less committed to the organization in the long term. I believe commitment is a gift you give yourself, because riding the fence and wavering in your commitment only means you're prolonging an inevitable fall, be it in your marriage or in your organizational life!

> There are too many people praying for mountains of difficulty to be removed when what they really need is courage to climb them.
> Anonymous

In the commitment to *New Growth* phase, we will finally begin to see teamwork come together. Our focus is once again on Others; but now, instead of being focused on what others are doing *to* us, we are focused on how we can partner with each other, build alliances, and work more effectively to support the big picture. Perhaps you are thinking why should I make a commitment to *New Growth,* when my organization is not making a 100% commitment to me? Because it is in **your** personal best interest to do so.

When you only give part of yourself to success in your job, you are asking for failure. It means constantly updating your resume and looking for other options. Remember, the grass is always greener on the other side of the fence, but it still needs to be mowed over there. If you think you're going to leave your current organization for a less tumultuous organization, in most cases, you will be in for a rude awakening. Nowadays, change in organizations is the norm, not the exception.

How would our world be different if we were all 100% committed to our marriages? How would your organization be different if all its employees were all 100% committed to the success of your organization? It would be much more difficult to fail. Instead of leaving your current organization, consider learning how to effectively cope with change. If you do this, you will learn skills that will last a lifetime.

PERSONAL APPLICATION QUESTIONS:

 Have you experienced a fear of the unknown with your organizational change? How do you cope with loss and pain?

 What phase in the *Cycle of Resistance* are you currently in/ how do you know?

 How has your organization communicated the change to its employees? What sources of information do you have to keep abreast of the changes? Are you familiar with the changes in your industry and the trends therein?

IF YOU'VE BEEN A CAT ALL DAY, YOU'LL BE A CAT AT NIGHT

"There was a change in my work job duties without asking me. I feel terrible, persecuted, punished for no apparent reason. I'm sure there are more changes to come. The boss is completely disengaged and not involved in what we do. He's always out, the only time we meet with him is when he likes us to take care of his needs or to let us know of dissatisfaction of a certain performance."

Director of Engineering

In April of 1996, after much discussion and thought, we decided that my husband Jim would quit his job. He had worked for the State of Ohio in Corrections for 12 years and was at the height of his career. He had just gotten the "Employee of the Quarter" award and had been selected to go to a big leadership program, indicating upper management thought he had management potential. Regardless, we decided that Jim would quit his job and come home to work with me, both to help with my speaking business and also play a larger role in raising our two young sons.

Initially we were excited about this. And even though I speak on change management, I did not anticipate that I would go through any resistance to this change. But I was caught off guard. I *ignored the pain* for maybe two or three weeks, and then suddenly it hit me. What have I done? I am now the sole breadwinner. Have I lost my mind? Why are we doing this? I felt tremendous stress and an increased burden to earn more money, to take on more training projects.

Suddenly it struck me: this is not going to be as easy as I thought it was. I very quickly moved into the *Feeling the Pain* phase. You need to know that this phase was not a pretty one for us. Why did I think I could work as a team with my husband when I never worked as a team player – on the basketball team or any other sport I ever participated in? I have always been a solo performer. I wanted all the responsibility **and** glory! At that point, I had been speaking for nine years, written two books, traveled the country, and did most everything for myself. Why did I think I would suddenly be able to accept being part of a partnership with my husband? Very quickly, I started to really *feel the pain*. I questioned how Jim fit in. What could he do to assist me? Could he do it as well as I did?

Although we had written out a job description for Jim before he quit, on one of Jim's first days at home, I told him, "Don't answer the phones." He asked why. I replied, "I'm sure you realize that clients and potential clients want to talk to **me** directly. They don't want to talk to you." Jim shrugged his shoulders.

What was I doing? I was telling Jim, "This is my job, and you had better not cross over." But I didn't stop there. I also told Jim that I had a great idea for what he could do — he could go to the post office and the copy store. Those two things would really help me out. Jim had the same reaction most of us would. He thought to himself..."I cannot believe I quit my job to go to the post office." To me, he grudgingly replied, "Okay, I can go to the post office and copy store." It was pretty evident that all I was giving Jim was the dirty work to do. Nothing team-oriented, nothing partnering-oriented.

The ironic thing is that I teach this, and I still didn't see what I was doing. My speaker friends noticed my natural reaction to pain long before I did. Jim did what most people do when they're dealing with people in pain: he tried to avoid me. This is difficult to do since we work out of our home. He had wanted to landscape our yard for about five years. So, he landscaped the whole yard. Then he hid in the basement workshop and organized it. He did anything to get some kind of gratification for himself because I was giving him no recognition or real part in the speaking business. Looking back, I recognize how painful and long those months were for us.

After several months of this, Jim turned to me one day and said,

"You know, Patti, I've observed something several times and I just want your feedback. I noticed that sometimes when people talk to you about the speaking business, you refer to it as 'our' business and then there are some days when you still refer to it as 'your' business. What gives?" I thought for a minute or two, and I said to him, "Well, it depends on what you did for me that day." Touche! My reaction was a classic reaction to pain that most of us experience. Some of us, however, don't recognize this reaction in ourselves.

People react like cats when they are in pain. To prove my point, let's compare cats to dogs. For those dog owners, when you go home at night and your dog hasn't seen you all day, what will your dog do when you come in the door? He gets all excited. Barks. Wags his tail. Jumps up on you.

In contrast to that, what does a cat do when you come home? Not much. If cats could talk, they'd be saying, "You're home? Ask me if I care." Cats keep to themselves. Unless you jiggle the cat food box of treats. They come immediately because there's something in it for them. That's exactly the same reaction that people have when they are in the "Feeling the Pain" phase in the Cycle of Resistance.

KEEP TO YOURSELF AND LICK YOUR WOUNDS

With this first reaction, most people don't communicate with each other. This makes everyone's job more difficult. If we would just talk with each other, the change would be easier. But we're upset. We're angry. We're feeling the pain . . . but we're not going to let you know.

Our initial inclination is to stay to ourselves and deal with the pain alone. We don't allow others to know about the pain we feel. Our internalized stress skyrockets; it begins to negatively affect our attitude and productivity. Often there is an increase in the level of silence and lack of communication, be it from one level of management to another level, between co-workers, or among departments.

"The members of this department did not feel valued and were discouraged from working as a team. They were also isolated from the rest of the organization by location and department practices. It has and will take some time to reintegrate our staff

with the others and to establish their value in their eyes as well
as with the rest of the organization."

Vice President of Community Services

Consider this...you have a dog which has gotten in a dog fight. Your dog comes limping to you. You've got to wash your dog off, brush him, baby him. Dogs are like little kids, right? However, with a cat, it can be days later until you notice your cat must have been in a fight. You didn't even know the cat was in a cat fight because she kept to herself and licked her wounds.

That is a very natural reaction of what people do in change: They keep to themselves and lick their wounds. You might say to a co-worker, "So, Jean, how are you doing with this departmental change?" Typically, she'll reply, "I'm fine." "Really, you seem to be a little . . . " "NO, I'm fine!" Fine is a wonderful word; it says a whole lot without saying much at all.

Back to my change with Jim working with me. I had people say to me, "So, how is it to have Jim working with you?" I always replied, "It's fine." It wasn't fine. I was in a tremendous amount of pain. I didn't know how to work as a team. I didn't like this part-nering thing. He didn't do things the way I wanted and not nearly as fast as I wanted it done. I was in pain, but doggone if I was going to tell anyone I was in pain. I kept to myself.

We need to find someone outside our organization with whom we can share our feelings. If you consistently keep to yourself, you are internalizing that stress. Internalized stress often manifests itself in physical symptoms or emotional turmoil. Find someone who is a good listener. A person with an objective viewpoint will be able to empathize with you but won't allow you to wallow in self-pity. Ask for their feedback about your situation. Allow yourself to vent, but don't stop with venting. Force yourself to come up with positive ways to deal with the changes.

WHINE AND MANIPULATE

A second natural reaction to your anger about the changes is to whine behind the boss's back to other people. You try to manipulate the system for your own agenda regardless of the impact on others. Morale in the organization drops.

Cats can be highly manipulative; they like working under-ground. It would be simpler and definitely more obvious if we were dogs. If people acted like dogs, they'd come and bark and yell and they'd really let you know how lousy this change was. As cats, we "whine and dine." We go out to lunch together, we whine and com-plain to each other about the changes. Can you believe they are making this change? and we go on and on about the problems of the changes and how it won't work. Back at work morale stinks because we're whining to each other. Rarely do we go to the boss with our comments because we don't believe she or he will understand. But we love to whine to co-workers and people in other departments because misery loves company.

🐾 *"While no significant changes to the way we do business have occurred to date, there has been a great deal of speculation and rumor-mongering that has occurred related to changes that may be coming. There is a lot of wasted energy being used to discuss the unknown."*

Supervisor

The potential of an uncertain future increases the stress in our lives. Naturally, rumors with accurate and inaccurate information are passed among all employees. Backstabbing is another form of whining and manipulating. By stabbing the leader in the back, I can manipulate him/her. Yet, what is critical for us is to feel more com-fortable with each other so we can gain trust in each other. We need to work at getting people off their own personal agenda and work-ing together toward this change. In chapter six, you will learn spe-cific techniques for how you can "whine with purpose" and tell the truth with love. Avoid spreading rumors; it will only further dis-courage you and others who listen to you. Use your words to heal, not hurt, others.

🐾 *"Administration is not good at communicating with the people below them. Professional and front-line people all need to feel informed, respected and important. Morale is really low right now. The changes were necessary and really belated. Management communicated poorly with people and information came out unofficially. People got the information second and*

third hand and with many half truths. By the time it got to all of
the employees, people were hurt and felt unimportant and
disrespected."

Support Coordinator

HISS AND PICK FIGHTS

We become aggressive and say things in anger. We no longer care about others' feelings. Our main goal becomes to make other people feel as miserable as we feel.

"My biggest concern is the unwillingness of the Executive
staff to admit they made a mistake. Some of them tend to point
out others' faults in an effort to minimize there own. This type of
behaviors causes resentment and animosity toward each other."

Director of Operations

This reaction can be dangerous, especially if it escalates. Employees mirror what they see happening at a management level. Occasionally I would pick fights with Jim over stupid, nitpicky things that really had no basis. I was miserable, yet couldn't figure out why. So, I just naturally picked fights because it's lonely to be miserable by yourself.

Step back from the situation and ask yourself, "Why am I picking fights with this person? Is my criticism of him/her legitimate? What is really going on here?" Have you noticed that you are having more spats and angry moments in your personal life? Has your stressed increased? Ask a trusted friend for their opinion of your behavior. Ask your significant other if and when they have noticed change(s) in your behavior at home. If they begin noticing changes at home, more than likely you are taking your work pain home with you. Develop a prearranged "secret signal" that a trusted co-worker or your significant other can give you when they see your negative behavior escalating. It is a signal for you to stop and make some choices about ending your negative reaction.

MARK YOUR TERRITORY

You know how cats mark their territory. People aren't much different. You decide you can't influence the entire team, so you'll just

You know how cats mark their territory. Humans are not that much different.

stick to your territory. You cover and protect any mistakes or problems in your department or area or responsibility. The departmental silos get more and more marked as we go through change.

Remember one of my initial reactions with Jim — "Don't answer the phone. I will answer the phone." I was marking my territory. This happens in organizations all the time. You'll hear comments like, "Change is fine as long as it doesn't affect my area. Don't think you're going to change my department."

"There have been mega changes in upper-level administration — president, provost, deans, vice presidents. Most all these people have come from 'the outside,' have no prior knowledge of or involvement with our institution, and many give evidence that this is, at best, a resume stop for them. It's a most unsettling feeling. The 'new guys' have no institutional history and seem uninterested in knowing any. They seem less interested in the university than in the impact they can have on the

institution. We have seen a lot of change for the sake of change ...
folks just wanting to 'mark their territory' if you will. The
institution was far from broken when they got here ... many of us
wish they'd stop trying to fix it!!"

Director

In some cases, employees mark their territory because they are jealous of others or feel threatened by others' abilities, knowledge, attitude. Regardless, everyone has their own agenda and seems to feel their department's needs and interests are more important than everyone else's. Be wary after surviving a reorganization of marking your territory by saying, "That's not my job!" A woman in a manufacturing plant said that very thing to her boss. To which her boss replied, "And it certainly never will be!" The boss made sure the woman never received any additional responsibilities OR promotions. Be careful of getting yourself stuck where you are now because of a territorial attitude.

A steel worker said that because there was no sharing of information at all levels, he felt like he was treated like a mushroom — "kept in the dark and fed B.S." He felt it was a direct result of people covering their territory due to total disregard for other areas in the company.

In fact, one of the major reasons corporate changes often fail is because of a lack of honesty between divisions or areas of the company. A top-level manager is paid on the results of his/her business unit, not necessarily on the results of the entire organization. Until pay is linked to entire team results, don't expect to see overall team unity.

WITHHOLD WARMTH

The final thing that we do is we withhold warmth. If you want to pet a cat and they don't want to be petted, you can*not* pet them. They merely arch their back, withhold their warmth, and they move on. People, in a very cat-like manner, don't actually withhold "warmth," they withhold something

> Cat's motto: No matter what you've done wrong, always try to make it look like the dog did it.
> Author Unknown

far more powerful in organizations today — information. Why? Information is power!

Managers can ask all the questions they want to, but we don't have to talk. Because if I have the information you don't have and you need it, you will fail, you will not get what you want. I can't control a lot of things within the organization, but I do have power over this!

Back to my story. I wouldn't tell Jim certain things. Why? Because then he'd fail and prove my point that this wasn't working out. It wasn't a conscious, vindictive desire to have others fail; it happens naturally in our resistance to painful change.

What is really difficult in this *Feeling the Pain* cat reaction is that you cannot herd cats. Likewise, have you ever heard the term "working cats"? No. "Working dogs"? Yes. There are guide dogs, sled dogs, hunting dogs. There is no such thing as "working cats." And in many organizations when employees are truly in this *Feeling the Pain* phase, employees are working just minimally to get by.

Information is power. Yet, often by not sharing information with the change leaders we are hurting ourselves. They will implement change with or without our input. When we refuse to give input, it usually translates to a less effective change. Freely give information. Ultimately, it may affect the way you do your job. It is far better to be a part of the change process than become a victim of it later on.

THE PERSONAL CHALLENGE TO CHANGE

The most important thing for you to realize in our natural reactions to change is this — if all day long you have been whining and manipulating, hissing and picking fights, withholding information and more . . . don't believe for a moment that you will magically transform yourself during the drive home. In actuality, here's what happens. If you have been acting like a cat all day long at work, you will come home and be a cat at night.

"The general feeling is one of negativity and distrust. Everyone feels like insignificant, unwanted, unappreciated minions that just deal with new requirements handed down to us without having our input honestly considered. Unfortunately, the

changes not only impact our jobs, but our personal lives as well."

Environmental Manager

The best reason I believe people should accept change and move forward is that it will benefit YOU! It is in our personal best interest to move on. Don't change for the company. Change for yourself. I'll never forget the big, burly steel worker who stayed after my program one day and wept, saying, "I lost my family because for three years I've gone home and acted like a cat every single night and my family is dead to me. I didn't even realize I was doing that to them."

We all take the pain home with us. When I realized this change was beginning to affect not only my business relationship with my husband, but my personal relationship with him as well, that's when I knew I had to stop myself from acting like a cat. I needed to move into the future for US. My speaking business probably would survive. But I needed to move forward for me and my marriage, so I made a conscious decision to move out of *feeling the pain* and into exploring how Jim and I could become partners in the business. It wasn't easy. It wasn't quick or without compromise on my part or Jim's. But it was absolutely worth it — both professionally and personally.

For those of you who are in pain, please recognize that your challenge is to move on for yourself and no one else. Move on for yourself because you will pay a heavy price personally if you choose not to move forward. These are choices that we make today which will affect us for years to come.

PERSONAL APPLICATION QUESTIONS:

 Have you counted the personal costs of the organizational change you are going through?

 What decisions and choices must you make in order to move forward in your changes?

 What objective, trustworthy person can give you honest feedback as to how you have been acting throughout this change?

PART II:

COMMUNICATION STRATEGIES TO UNTIE THE 'NOTS' IN ORGANIZATIONAL CHANGE

SHIVER ME TIMBERS...

🐚 *"I have changed locations, offices, and bosses. The biggest change is the supervisor situation. I am very unclear about my objectives, evaluation, vision or direction. I feel as though I'm swimming upstream and don't even know why. There appears to be little recognition of my past experience or the value I bring to my department."*

Associate Director

Julie had been the Assistant Vice President of Human Resources for six years when a new Vice President arrived. Julie was particularly excited because her new boss was a woman. Perhaps she could mentor Julie? Julie hoped to establish a great relationship from the start. At the beginning, their relationship flourished. But after several months a tension grew, and distrust developed. The new VP was making enormous changes within the organization. Some of these changes Julie felt that she should have been consulted on. The organizational ship had been smoothly sailing along prior to this VP's arrival. Did an entire new ship need to be built? Gradually the new VP felt more to Julie like a pirate that had jumped aboard ship rather than a captain who cared about the shipmates.

Julie's experience is like many of us who get a new boss or leader. We excitedly anticipate new leadership . . . until the person arrives and starts making changes. Most of us feel that our organization is smoothly sailing along. When a new leader comes on board, it's as if a pirate has jumped aboard our organizational ship, and now the whole ship is rocking. Shiver me timbers . . .

"First impressions have already been made in the merger. Many of us feel as though we are being treated as an inferior company, a conquered province...I feel we are being treated as though this was a hostile takeover rather than a merger. The communication I have received is given in the context of a command rather than best practices."

Computer Help Desk Technician

Often when there have been a significant number of changes in personnel, especially at the senior level, we perceive that there is no attempt by these new leaders to integrate into "our" community. At times we feel that these "pirate leaders" are making change for "change's sake." There can be a sense among long-term employees that the new leaders do not have a strong commitment to the true mission of our organization. With public sector/not-for-profit orga-

When a new leader comes on board, it's as if a pirate has jumped aboard our organizational ship, and now the whole ship is rocking.

nizations in particular, we perceive that the leaders are moving toward a "corporate"-type structure . . . a "race for the bottom line." This creates a sense among employees that the new administrators have no "respect" for the long, rich institutional history, and that little attention is being paid to the organization's core values.

> "We have moved to a less personal and more corporate model, one that has emphasized top-down decisions rather than a mutual problem-solving and decision-making model. Staff sometimes learn of decisions that are made rather than being asked to participate in the process of decision making. While I think these changes have been with good intentions, they have hurt us."
>
> *Counselor*

Most of us want to feel somewhat grounded in our job. Although we know that nothing is permanent, and changes do happen, we would like to have some kind of anchor. Research indicates that 85% of employees quit due to conflicts in the boss-employee relationship. In a Robert Half International survey, executives were found to spend a month per year dealing with personality conflicts. This may explain why employers place more value on the candidate's personality than any other factor during the hiring process. Since the boss-employee relationship is such a tenuous one, how can we best manage that relationship?

BUILDING TRUST WITH YOUR BOSS

Trust is the key to success in any organization. The way to develop trust is by building respect for individual differences. In a trust relationship a person can relate to another's interests even when they disagree. The relationship is based on mutual understanding instead of mutual dependency.

We need to recognize that the boss-employee relationship is not like the parent-child relationship in that the burden of managing the relationship does not fall entirely on the boss. In managing this relationship as employees, we have three basic choices: (1) to change our boss, (2) to change our environment, or (3) to change ourselves. We have the most control over ourselves, yet we seem to search for ways to change or blame our boss or the environment when things change. It's important to recognize that we can rarely change our boss; and if we are not willing to change our environment, the most likely option we have is to change ourselves.

> Trust is the key to success in any organization. The way to develop trust is by building respect for individual differences.

Most of us grew up with the *Golden Rule of Success*, which is: "Do unto others as you would have them do unto you." Has it ever irritated you when people at work don't seem to reciprocate and treat you the way you want to be treated? Isn't that the way it's supposed to work? The *Golden Rule* works effectively with customers, but there is a better rule for us to apply at work — particularly with a new boss — the *Platinum Rule of Success*.

Dr. Tony Alessandra developed and wrote a book about the Platinum Rule of Success: "Do unto others as they would like to be done unto." In other words, treat people the way they want to be treated. This implies that we must know something about the other person in order to treat them the way they want to be treated.

How many of you work with someone who is completely opposite of you? How many of you are in a significant relationship in which the person is opposite? You know the saying — "opposites attract." I often find that "opposites attack." Jim and I have been married since 1983, and we definitely fit the "opposites attract" model. For the first ten years of our marriage, I would often pray, "Lord, help Jim to listen to me and change — he could be so much better if he would do what I say." It took ten years of Jim not changing and me getting frustrated to realize I married him in the first place because he brought things to our relationship that I was lacking. In this next decade of our marriage, I pray daily to love Jim as he is. We've developed a very strong relationship as a result of me changing my perspective. How many of you can relate to that?

I once read two "Peanuts" cartoon strips that perfectly depict the differences between Jim and me. Jim is a lot like Peppermint Patty. She is about to take a test. She raises her hand and asks the teacher, "On this test, ma'am, do you want our last name first or our first name first? How about a middle initial? Should we put down a middle initial? Okay, I gotcha. Not used to dealing with a perfectionist, hum, ma'am?" Jim is a perfectionist. He has lists and files for everything, and he absolutely loves the Internet because he can research just about anything before buying or making a decision.

On the other hand, I am much more like Sally, who turns to her brother, Charlie Brown, for advice on a school project. She says, "I have to do a book report on *Treasure Island*, do you know what it's about?" Charlie replies, "It's about pirates." "That's all I need to know," says Sally. "I can fake the rest of it." I'm a big-picture person who loves to focus on vision and ideas for the future. I don't like getting bogged down in details. The only exception is that I am extremely detailed when researching and customizing programs for my speaking clients. But in my personal life, I hate to be bothered with minutia.

This difference was brought home for me several years ago. At the time, Jim was running, for fitness reasons, and one of his favorite treats after running was frozen green grapes. Frozen green grapes are wonderful, natural, sweet, frozen treats — excellent for refreshment after a hot activity. There is, however, one small problem with frozen green grapes — after you wash them and put them into the freezer, they can develop icicles on the outside. I never gave this a second thought, but obviously Jim had.

I came home from a speaking engagement one evening and Jim met me at the door exclaiming, "I had a great idea at work today!" I immediately assumed he had come up with a visionary idea. I excitedly replied, "Great! What was your idea?" Jim said, "You remember that problem with the frozen green grapes?" I blindly asked, "What problem with the frozen green grapes?" Jim impatiently said, "The icicle problem!" "The icicle problem?" I incredulously said. "Yes, the icicle problem!" Jim proudly relayed his great idea. "I stopped by the grocery store on my way home from work and bought some green grapes. When I got home, I took the grapes off the stem, washed them in the sink, and laid the grapes out on a towel. Here's my great idea (I could hardly wait to hear it) — I went upstairs, opened the bathroom closet door, took out your blowdryer, came downstairs, and blew the grapes dry."

My mouth dropped. I was stunned. "You blew the grapes dry?" I asked. Later I realized how we are created so differently from one another. What excites one person may not necessarily be the best idea for another.

If we are to be effective in our professional and personal lives, we need to learn what motivates and drives other people, and then treat them the way they want to be treated.

Let's apply that concept to your new pirate leader. One key to understanding and managing the relationship with our boss is to try and understand what makes our boss "tick." What are the boss's pet peeves? How do you know they are angry? satisfied? In presenting your ideas to your boss, are they interested in all the details or just the bottom line? Do they prefer competition or cooperation?

Often, we present ourselves and our ideas as we would like them to be presented to us, when in fact, the key to managing someone is to try to best meet their needs, not ours. Observe someone who really seems to get along with your boss — what does that person do to be so successful? Often we are too close to the relationship to be objective, but by observing someone else, we gain ideas we can use in the relationship.

BUILDING RAPPORT TO GET RESULTS

In understanding and building a relationship with our new leader, is it more important to be a good *sender* of information or *receiver*? When working for a new person, it is initially more important to listen than it is to speak. How else will we really get to know him/her and be able to treat them the way they want to be treated?

Is there an art to being a good listener? Absolutely. Does it come naturally? I don't think so. In fact, there was some interesting research that indicates that we hear half of what is said, listen to half of what we hear, understand half of it, believe half of that, and remember only half of that.

Let me translate that for you into an eight-hour workday; it means:

- You spend about 4 hours listening.
- You hear about 2 hours' worth.
- You actually listen to 1 hours' worth.
- You understand 30 minutes of that hour.
- You believe only 15 minutes' worth; and
- You remember just under 8 minutes' worth.

Tom Peters, author of *In Search of Excellence,* says, "Good listeners get out from behind their desk to where the customers are." Do you get out from behind your desk and give your full attention to your boss when s/he talks to you? If not, let me provide you with a cutting-edge technique that will improve your listening with your boss as well as help you gain rapport with anyone you meet. This technique is extremely powerful because it works at a subconscious level. This technique comes from the science of Neuro Linguistics Programming/NLP.

Before I explain the technique, let me give you some background information that will help you see its potential power. One communication barrier is the fact that we sometimes fake attention. This is due in part to our Thought/Speech Ratio. Most people speak at a rate of about 150 words per minute. We can think, listen, and process about 500 words per minute. We literally have the ability to process information 4-5 times faster that the other person's talking. Most people only give half-hearted attention to their boss while s/he is speaking.

A research study was conducted to determine how important the nonverbal aspects of communication are compared to the actual words we use when communicating one-on-one. If you divide interpersonal communication into the *Words* we use, the *Tone of Voice*, and *Gestures* or Body Language, what percentages would you give to each? The following conclusions were made: Your words are 7% of your communication, your tone of voice is credited with 38%, and your gestures are equivalent to 55% of your total communication.

The surprising reality is that much of the communication training centers around the use of words. Since the nonverbal component is so important, that is what we are going to concentrate on. Let's explain what Neuro Linguistics Programming is and why it is so powerful.

In short, **NLP,** developed by John Grinder and Richard Bandler, is a system that allows us to "read" people more sensitively and respond to them more effectively (i.e., treat them the way they want to be treated). We are able to establish a positive relationship quickly by incorporating NLP into the way we work with people.

Neuro stands for your nervous system or non-verbal behavior. Everything in your nervous system runs subconsciously. Most times, you are not consciously aware of what you are doing nonverbally. The way you typically sit is probably not consciously chosen. You sit the way you've always sat. It is subconscious and natural.

Linguistics stands for your language. In this case, your nonverbal language.

Programming is just like a computer program. It is a program you put into place to achieve a specific result. With this technique we are looking to build rapport with other people.

Mirroring, which is one of several NLP techniques, is the art of copying another person's behavior to create a relaxed communication situation, the reason being that we like people who are like us. "Birds of a feather flock together." If we like someone, we trust them AND want to do business with them. Think about the potential this has for building a business relationship with your boss. It also has implications for your social relationships and friendships.

Specifically, this is how you mirror:

First, match the other person's *voice tone or tempo*. If they talk fast, you talk fast. If they talk slowly, you talk slowly. When I speak in New York, I can't speak quickly enough. If I'm in southern Texas, I slow my pace down to match their pace. One way to help you match the other person's tempo is to pace yourself to the other person's breathing rate.

Match the other person's *body movements, posture, and gestures.* If your boss crosses his/her legs, you cross your legs. If they use gestures, you gesture. Of course, subtlety is everything. You may want to wait several seconds before moving. A very important point about gesturing is that we only gesture when we speak. This won't make much sense to you until you go out and observe other people speaking to each other. But trust me, this is important to keep in mind.

Please know that you do not need to mirror a person's every move. Be selective. A client once told me that her boss picked her nose — did she need to do the same? Of course not. Be as natural as possible. You will find that you actually "feel" the same way the person you are speaking to feels — because you are mirroring their nonverbal behaviors, which is a reflection of their feelings.

The process of mirroring is totally natural. You do it naturally with people you like and have built rapport with. Have you ever coincidentally noticed that you and a friend simultaneously scratched your noses at the same time? It's mirroring, it's just that you didn't know that is what it is called.

Author and Marriage/Family Counselor Morton Kelsey said it well when he said, "Listening is being silent in an active way." Think of it this way: Rearranging the letters in the word listen creates "silent." How much more effective would we be with our boss if we would listen more and talk less? Just envision the level of rapport and trust that can be built with the simple act of mirroring your boss.

READILY PROVIDE INFORMATION

We need to focus positively on the new vision that might come about from the change in leadership. If your new leader provides open "chat sessions," attend and ask questions. Readily provide input, even when not asked. Once you have a feel for your leader's likes and dislikes, provide information to him/her in a manner that fits their style. Examples of information you can provide may include a brief historical overview of your unit or job function, examples of money you have saved the organization, major projects you have spearheaded, or recommendations of quality-improvement ideas or ways to improve efficiency.

One warning: Be careful not to appear like a "brown-noser" to your colleagues or over-eager to your new boss. Simply provide information in a professional manner that the new leader might find useful. This is your chance to influence the future direction of your department and area of responsibility. Don't leave it to fate.

Another way to provide information is to volunteer to serve on committees which are dealing directly with the change process. Don't be a whiner behind the scenes — no leader likes that. Be a part of the change process by becoming a change agent rather than falling prey to the victim mentality.

KEEP GOING AND GROWING

Keep upgrading your technical and nontechnical skills. Professionals who are committed to life long learning don't put their life "on hold" when a new leader arrives.

This may be a great time to examine the ways to get rid of reports or work that may no longer be valuable to your organization. Learn how to analyze problems, be creative, and find solutions. Don't become comfortable with the status quo.

Be sure you are coachable when the new leader comes to you with a change in duties or criticizes the way you do your job. For specific ideas on how to become more open to criticism, read the next chapter on *The Thrill of Victory, The Agony of Criticism.* Once an idea is introduced and you don't like the idea, then it is time to read through Chapter Six so you can learn how to "whine with purpose."

> ✪ *"I've had to go through a grieving process with the leadership changes. As much as I "understand" the reasons behind the reorganization, I still find it hard to "live out" some of these changes on a daily basis. I don't feel like I'm opposed to change for the most part. I just had an unusually close relationship with my previous supervisor for 15 years. It's hard to lose that. Not that it can't happen again. It's hard sometimes not to 'look in the rear view mirror.' "*
>
>   *Assistant to the Dean of Students*

You may need to give yourself some time to "mourn" the fact that you no longer work for your former boss. Recognize the fact that the arrival of a new leader may signal an opportunity for a significant direction change. Know that positioning yourself as an opponent to the new leader is usually the "kiss of death" and is rarely a winning plan. Therefore, consider positioning yourself on the side of the boss to become a partner in the organization's success.

CASE STUDY: MEET YOUR NEW BOSS LADY

Here is a true case study (the names are changed to protect the innocent) with specific recommendations on how to deal with a new boss. I hope you find the suggestions helpful.

SITUATION

When a new president comes on board, excitement and apprehension go hand in hand. The arrival of the new president to Middle State University was met with great excitement. As the new leader, he appointed all new Vice Presidents to his cabinet.

The Vice President selected for the Business and Fiscal Affairs division quickly implemented some changes in the way her division conducted business. Some of her expectations included: preparing trend analyses rather than just producing numbers on the fiscal reports, and the implementation of business process improvement for the paper flow in the entire division. Her main goal was to have people think for themselves rather than having someone give them step-by-step instructions of what to do as was previously the norm.

The new VP's style was met with fear (for job security), mistrust of her motives, and frustration at having to change the way staff had always done their job (have we done everything wrong all these years?). She tried to keep the communication channels open by writing a monthly division newsletter and hosting division-wide informal chats. These efforts were met with a lukewarm response.

After discussions with the Assistant Vice President for Human Resources, it was agreed to bring in Patti Hathaway to do some confidential focus groups in order to develop a full-day training program for the management team and a half-day training session for the rest of the division's staff. As a result of the success of the programs delivered in the Business and Fiscal Affairs division, Patti Hathaway was asked to conduct a two-day retreat for the President and Deans to assist them in building more effective partnerships. This new emphasis on training and development for the staff was met with enthusiasm, and attitudes began to change for the better.

RECOMMENDATIONS

Management Strategies: If you are the new boss, here are some strategies for you to consider.

1) Ease the number of changes being implemented simultaneously.

2) Avoid making comparisons to previous organizations you have worked for and previous employees.

3) Copy your staff on articles which discuss your industry's trends and changes.

4) Encourage management and line staff to attend industry conferences and continue to upgrade their skills.

5) Involve staff in providing input for reorganization recommendations.

Employee Strategies: If you are an employee in a similar situation with a new boss, here are some strategies for you to consider.

1) Attend the Vice President's chat sessions and ask questions and provide input.

2) Keep upgrading your technical and non-technical skills. Professionals are committed to continual learning.

3) Look for ways to get rid of reports or work that is no longer valuable to your institution.

4) Volunteer to serve on committees which are dealing directly with the change process.

5) Learn how to analyze problems, be creative, and find solutions. Do not become comfortable with the status quo.

PERSONAL APPLICATION IDEAS:

 Observe the interactions your boss has with other people. Specifically note if the boss is interested in lots of details or just the bottom line. Does s/he prefer competition or cooperation? What are the boss's pet peeves? How do you know when they are angry?

 In your next one-on-one meeting, make a conscious choice to mirror your new boss. What did you learn about them by "acting" (mirroring) just like them? Do they tend to be low-key or easily excitable? Do they prefer thinking before speaking or do they quickly draw their conclusions?

 What information would be important to a new leader in your organization? In what format would your boss most appreciate this information? Be proactive and get the information and provide it to them as a way of partnering with them.

THE THRILL OF VICTORY, THE AGONY OF CRITICISM

"The people that are fearful of change will usually bad-mouth the product, the technology, the people that have worked with it. They will become defensive and narrow minded and simply not willing to accept the change whether it's the best thing every to happen to them. Help rid the fear that people have that really is the enemy of change, the fear of the unknown."

Data Software Manager

I learned about being coachable while playing three years of varsity basketball in high school. If you're six feet tall, you had better do something useful with your height. It's important for you to know that my greatest regret when I graduated from high school is that I was never voted "The Most Valuable Player" (MVP) in basketball... and I WAS the most valuable player in basketball! I scored the most points. I had the most rebounds. I had all the statistics that should have rendered me the Most Valuable Player award. However, I didn't play like a team player. I was interested only in my own statistics. As a result, my teammates purposefully did not vote me as the MVP. I was devastated when as a senior, a junior player was voted MVP.

In hindsight, I recognize now that I shouldn't have received the MVP. Not only was I only interested in my statistics, I also wasn't very coachable. Through the years, I had numerous coaches try to teach me how to shoot a "set shot." I always shot with two hands. For the non-basketball readers, kids stop shooting with two hands in about the third grade. A set shot is a much more accurate shot, one more difficult to defend.

My coach would say, "You know, Patti, if you would just learn to shoot a set shot, you could be so much better." My reply? I'd say, "I'm already the best player you have. Talk to the rest of the players and see why they aren't scoring more. If they'd get better, we'd have a good team." In other words, I was already good and...totally uncoachable! The question is, how coachable are you? How willing are you to change your job and the way you work?

When someone suggests to you, "Have you ever thought about doing your job this way? How about applying the new technology in your job function? Would you consider doing this task slightly differently?" Do you quickly reply, "I already do a fine job!"

You know what I find interesting? Change is fine as long as it doesn't affect me. We have the attitude that change is great — for other people. They are the ones who need to change, not me. My guess is that many of you are no different than I was. A lot of people going through change are totally uncoachable.

You'd be really impressed to see what I won after three years of playing varsity basketball. A little, tiny trophy inscribed with my name and the words "3 year award." It's quite impressive. The coaches made this award up because they had never had a player who played varsity basketball for three years and who wasn't selected as the most valuable player. It just didn't happen. I liken my "three-year award" to going to the Miss America Pageant and getting voted "Miss Congeniality." Really nice, but not the ultimate award. That's what my award says to me. The truth is that I didn't deserve the most valuable player award and neither do you if you are uncoachable in change situations.

THE "MOST VALUABLE PLAYER" SYNDROME

Unfortunately, this *MVP Syndrome* is what happens in many organizations, especially those going through change. When people are concerned about their job security, they inevitably ask themselves, "Am I going to lose my job? Am I going to be replaced? Am I going to be outsourced? Is my function going to be outsourced?" Those questions automatically create tremendous fear. We naturally fear the unknown and often will move into actions that speak loudly the message, "Well, I'm going to show everyone that I'm the most valuable player so if the company is going to replace somebody, it

We try to show everyone that we're the "most valuable player" so if the company is going to replace somebody, it won't be us.

won't be me."

For example, if Curt and I work for two different companies that have merged, and both hold the same position in the different companies, it's obvious there's really only work for one of us. Don't you think I'm going to make myself look good and make Curt look bad because that way the boss who has to make the decision as to which one stays and which one leaves will decide in my favor? Patti wins. Curt loses. I win the elusive MVP award. But what happens to team effectiveness? I have seen companies and departments paralyzed by internal dissension and in-fighting because they are all trying to vie for this most valuable player. There is inherently little teamwork in organizational change.

BECOMING COACHABLE

Being coachable and receiving criticism is a difficult yet essential skill for each one of us to master when going through change.

Inevitably, our jobs and job duties will change. One of the most important steps to becoming more coachable is learning how to deal with criticism. By opening ourselves to criticism, we can learn how to improve ourselves profes-

> *Show me a thoroughly satisfied man and I will show you a failure.*
> Thomas Edison

sionally (and personally). If we are completely satisfied with where we are and are not willing to accept criticism, we probably will not proceed much further in our careers nor experience much growth and satisfaction in our lives.

Charles Spurgeon once said, "Insults are like bad coins; we cannot help their being offered to us, but we need not take them." It is good to realize as the recipient of criticism that we have more control than the critic, once the criticism has been delivered. It is then up to us to decide whether we believe the criticism has merit and is worth acting upon.

PREPARATION FOR CRITICISM

There are basically three stages we experience when preparing for criticism. Stage 1 is the Awareness stage, Stage 2 is the Assessment stage, and Stage 3 is the Action stage. Let's look at each one of these stages a little more closely.

In the AWARENESS stage, we obviously realize that we are being criticized and our natural instincts take over. We may respond by counterattacking and becoming defensive, OR we may become a silent victim and automatically accept the criticism at face value.

Let's look at the pros and cons of these two instinctive responses. When we counterattack our critic, we often do so with sarcasm, put downs, or digs. I'm often amazed at how often people attend my "Dealing with Difficult People" workshops merely looking for the quick put-downs or counterattacks. In fact, sometimes, our one-liners are real "zingers," and, if we have an audience, we may get a big laugh out of them. Someone once told me that the Greek translation for sarcasm is "tear flesh." It is an excellent word picture for the damage sarcasm brings to the criticized. We will use our words to hurt or to heal.

 "After working for over a year to try and change the management philosophy and attitudes of the main office, I

became frustrated. I began taking a more win/lose
confrontational approach. Although I was extremely successful
in getting their attention, it was probably a bad idea in the long
run. Now they see me as a tremendous threat to doing things the
way we have always done it. I am now desperately trying to
change that win/lose mentality but that will obviously be
extremely difficult at this point."

District Office Manager

Comedians and cartoonists use sarcasm a lot because the comments can be very funny. For example, "My wife started to diet when she went from a size 9 to a size tent." Although it's a funny statement, it cuts to the heart of the person being put down.

The downside of counterattacking is obvious. You have not helped to build a relationship but instead have resorted to putting your critic down. This does not promote a climate in which you can comfortably continue to talk with your critic, nor your critic with you. It certainly does not show a willingness to be coached.

Imagine a player counterattacking his/her coach when the coach criticizes them. A coach's job is to teach and instruct. The player's job is to listen to the coach and apply what they learned in their game. Counterattacking has no place on the playing field or in the game of life.

When we counterattack an aggressive critic, we may think we are not affecting that person. However, our critic may not be as thick-skinned as we might have imagined. Often, critical people are as insecure as people who behave passively.

The silent victim or passive approach is no more helpful. If you say nothing or accept the criticism as valid before assessing it, you will appear to have little self-confidence and may lose the respect of others and yourself! Secondly, you may not truly understand what the critic intended by the criticism unless you take time to assess the criticism.

The point is to not automatically assume your critic is right nor to automatically change your behavior. A far better approach to handling criticism is to be aware that criticism is "just criticism" and then move quickly to assessing its merit.

In stage 2, you ASSESS how the criticism was delivered, the intent of the critic, and how valid you believe the criticism to be. It

is at this point that you may want to
ask yourself a couple of questions to
determine whether or not the criticism
is valid:

> *A man who trims him-self to suit everybody will soon whittle himself away.*
>
> Charles Schwab

1. Do I hear the same criticism
   from other people?
2. Does the "coach" know a great
   deal about this topic?
3. Are the coach's standards known and reasonable?
4. Is the criticism really about me, or is the critic merely hav-ing a bad day or upset about something else?
5. How important is it for me to be coachable in this situation?

Watch also for the nonverbal behavior of your critic. You may be able to determine the intensity of his or her feelings and how open he or she will be to the action you decide to take.

In the final stage, you decide what ACTION, if any, you want to take with the criticism. Let's examine some ACTION strategies for dealing assertively with the criticism.

BECOMING COACHABLE WITH CRITICISM

If we can be coachable while being criticized, it will allow us to remain confident and cool. A coachable and assertive approach per-mits a "win-win" attitude in which you allow your critic to have an opinion while maintaining your own. Manuel J. Smith, author of *When I Say No, I Feel Guilty,* introduces three assertive techniques which I have adapted. These techniques have proven to be invalu-able in helping assess and evaluate what action to take when being criticized. Keep in mind that the goal is to become coachable in order to become better at what you do. The three techniques are: Fogging, Admitting the Truth, and Asking for Specific Feedback. We will review each of these techniques by examining the situation and types of criticism with which they are most effective.

The first thing we must do when someone criticizes us invalidly or unjustifiably is to set up a psychological barrier that protects us from taking the criticism personally. One of the foundations for han-dling criticism effectively is self-confidence and high self-esteem. If we believe in ourselves, in our abilities, skills, and knowledge, then the criticism is much less threatening, and we tend to take it less personally. The bottom line is that we must choose to let the criticism have no devastating impact.

DEALING WITH UNJUSTIFIED CRITICISM AND ADVICE

The first criticism technique is ideal for dealing with unjustified criticism. When you receive this type of criticism, force yourself to avoid the natural reaction of counter-criticizing or counter-manipulating your critic. We often receive this type of criticism in the form of advice — often both unwarranted and unasked for!

An example might be a new boss who overhears you on the phone with a customer and says, "Boy, I just overheard you on the phone with that customer. I'm not sure that is the approach you should have taken."

Naturally, there are two ways to respond to your boss: (1) mumble and/or admit that we were wrong (a passive approach); or (2) tell the boss where they could go with their opinion (the aggressive route). A far better approach would be to utilize the assertive FOGGING technique, which calmly acknowledges that there MAY be some truth in the criticism.

What fogging does is allow you to receive the criticism without becoming anxious or defensive. It allows you to be the final judge of what to do about it. You become a listener instead of a reader of minds. The result is like a fog bank: you are unaffected by manipulative, unjustified criticism. After a while, your critic finds it's no fun to throw things at you.

For the previous criticism of your new boss, you could fog them by saying, "Perhaps I could've responded to the customer differently." You don't say to the critic that they are absolutely right, and you don't tell them they are absolutely wrong. You merely agree that there may be some truth in the statement. Other potential fogging responses might begin with: You might be right about . . . You could be right about . . . What you say makes sense . . .

One of the criticisms my mom likes to give me is the need for me to take more vitamins. Because I travel with my speaking business, have contact with lots of people, and have two young boys at home, I do occasionally get a cold during the winter. My mom's advice to me goes something like this, "Patti, I think you should take more vitamin C. You know, just the other day I read in *Prevention* magazine that if you take 20,000 megadoses of vitamin C per day, you'll have 60% fewer colds a year."

Admittedly, my natural response to my mother would go something like this . . . "Oh, Mother, you know vitamin C has little to do with the common cold." Well, you can imagine what would happen as a result . . . we would have a major argument about vitamin C and the pros and cons of taking it. Is this worth arguing about? No.

So what I do instead is to use a Fogging Response like . . . "Maybe I should take more vitamin C." And then I change the subject. My mom isn't sure what just happened. Did I agree with her or disagree? It's like being surrounded by a fog bank. I move on before the fog has a chance to clear. Meanwhile, after the conversation, I can decide whether or not I want to take vitamin C.

It's important to note that often unjustified criticism is expressed in broad, general terms which are unrealistic, untrue, and often spoken out of anger. When encountering criticism, watch out for words like "always," "never," "all the time," and "every time." Many times, this indicates the criticism is unjustified and a fogging response is appropriate.

Let's look at a couple of more examples of unjustified criticism and potential fogging responses:

"You're always late."	"Perhaps I am a bit late this time."
"Every time you are told about an error, you get defensive."	"You might be right about my tendency to get defensive. I don't like it when I make errors."

An easy mistake for people to make with the fogging technique is to "Yes, but . . ." That is, to make a good fogging statement and then add on the reasons why they did what they did. Take the previous example. "Yes, I am late, *but* I've been working on the report you assigned me two days after the deadline . . ." A good fogging statement uses active listening skills to paraphrase the criticism but doesn't add any excuses or rationalizations.

One of my participants in a communication program for a manufacturing client, Joe, was a shipping and receiving employee. He was incessantly teased about the size of his nose and how it got in the way of his work. Joe's typical response was to get physically violent. He would run the hi-low machine into wooden storage crates and punch boxes with his fists. His coworkers loved the reaction they got out of Joe by teasing him about something he could not change (unless, of course, he opted for plastic surgery!). I mean, how many of us have control over the size of our nose?

You get the picture. Well, Joe decided that he would employ the fogging technique the next time he was teased about the size of his nose. I have to admit, even I wasn't sure it would work with these tough guys. This is how Joe responded to his co-workers' jibes. Teasing comment — "Joe, would you mind moving, we can't see the load when your nose is in the way." Joe would fog them by saying, "Perhaps my nose is blocking your view. Let me move for you." After about a week of fogging, Joe reported to the class that his co-workers said to him, "What are you learning in that class? You know, you're not much fun anymore." One result of Joe's fogging was that his critics found him less fun to criticize.

> It is not the critic who counts. The credit actually belongs to the man in the arena, whose face is marred by dust and sweat and blood — who at best knows in the end the triumph of high achievement, and who at worst, if he fails, at least fails while daring greatly, so that his place will never be with those cold and timid souls who know neither victory nor defeat."
> Theodore Roosevelt

One of the greatest benefits to fogging is that it forces you to listen to your critic instead of automatically reacting to his/her comments. The result is that you are becoming more coachable in the process. Secondly, after you have handled the situation, you can decide whether or not the criticism has any merit and whether or not you want to take any action. In Joe's case, he decided that fogging was a lot less expensive and painful than nose surgery!

If you choose NOT to use the fogging technique, then you have several other options: You can grin and bear it. You can ignore it (but watch out for your nonverbal reactions, which may give away your true feelings). Or you can disagree politely. Always keep in mind that when handling unjustified criticism, you need to consider the critic. To what degree is the criticism a reflection of your critic's personality and motivation? Are they really trying to be helpful in coaching you, or do they have other motives?

Consider when using the fogging technique that there is always room for more than one opinion. Rarely is anything so black and white that it is worth arguing about. The goal of fogging is to stop the criticism. Later, you can decide whether or not to do something about the situation that provoked the criticism in the first place.

DEALING WITH VALID CRITICISM

The second technique of ADMITTING THE TRUTH is very effective when handling *valid criticism*. That is, accept your mistakes and faults without overapologizing for them. Too often when we make a mistake we try and cover it up. Perhaps the root of coverups lies in our childhood of getting "caught" and our fear of punishment. But in reality, the best thing we can do is to admit we made a mistake and move on.

When you admit the truth, it desensitizes you to criticism from yourself or others. It allows you to recognize mistakes as mistakes. The result is that once you accept your mistakes, you can move forward rather than become bogged down in depression and self-criticism. It also helps extinguish the criticism.

Potential replies to valid criticism might include: "You're right, I didn't get the report in on time." "You're right. I did do that incorrectly. Now that I know the correct way to do it, I'll get it finished." The key here is to not *over*apologize.

Additional things to think about when responding to valid criticism include:

- Focus on the present, not the past.
- Accept responsibility for the mistake but don't indulge in self put-downs.
- Avoid denying, counter-criticizing, overapologizing, or overcompensating. You need to agree with the specifics of your mistake.
- Assess if there is anything you can do NOW about the situation, and work to negotiate a compromise.

DEALING WITH VAGUE CRITICISM

The last type of criticism is *vague criticism*. This is sometimes the most difficult and frustrating type of criticism. In these cases, it is important to REQUEST SPECIFIC FEEDBACK. Listen to your critic and ask specific questions. With the use of questions, you can begin focusing on the future instead of dwelling on the past. It moves you directly into the ACTION stage and forces the critic to look at potential solutions instead of belaboring your failure. Also, it enlists the critic to be on your side.

Requesting specific feedback helps you to gain information you can use. As well, you exhaust your critic's complaints and often uncover the critic's true feelings and discover common ground. The result is that you break the manipulative cycle of criticism by improving understanding and communication. Some examples include: What did I specifically do that was a problem? . . . How could I improve my performance? . . . I'm not sure I'm clear about what your perception of the problem is. Could you please give me some examples?

All of these questions will force the critic to be clearer, more precise, and will enable you to change your behavior to more effectively meet their expectations or needs. A sports player cannot excel without a coach's clear and specific instructions on what to do to improve, nor can we improve without clear feedback.

The whole idea behind this technique is to reduce the vague criticism to manageable, behavioral terms. You want to prompt your critic to be specific. Don't become defensive, counter-critical, or immediately deny the criticism. Instead, try to be genuine in your desire to receive information. It may even be helpful to repeat or paraphrase your understanding of the critic's statements.

The basic skills of admitting the truth and requesting specific feedback will help to extinguish the criticism and enable you to assess whether or not there is anything you can do about the situation. It also moves you directly into the ACTION stage, where you can take steps to correct the mistake or negotiate a compromise.

Let's look at a couple of examples of vague criticism and how you might want to respond. "The report you turned in was really sloppy." "What, specifically, did you find sloppy about the report?" or "You're not very much of a team player, are you?" "What makes

A true professional learns how to build a firm foundation out of the bricks that other people throw at them.

you think I'm not a team player?"

It is essential when questioning a vague critic to make sure that you use a neutral tone of voice and body language. Let's redo one of the previous examples by using a tone of voice that sends a very different message. "You're not very much of a team player, are you?" "What makes YOU think I'M not a TEAM player?" It's not only the words you use but how you say them that makes all the difference in the world in how your questions will be received. Always be genuine.

Let me give you a couple of examples to see how you might respond using the skills we've outlined so far. #1: Your manager wants to pull you off a project you have been working on for two months and give it to another person in your department. You think you have been doing a good job and want to complete the project. How will you approach your manager, and what will you say since s/he has not criticized your work directly?

You might want to say, "I'm concerned that you are pulling me off of project X and giving it to Janet. Is there any particular reason for the change?" By requesting specific feedback, you should get to the reasons behind the change.

#2: At your last performance appraisal, your boss told you that you could be doing a "better job." You want to ask her to be more specific, but you also know that she doesn't like to be put on the spot. How will you do this?

Your response might include, "I appreciated your feedback at my performance appraisal meeting last week. After spending some time with the evaluation, I noticed that you wrote that I could be doing a "better job" in project management. Could you give me some specific suggestions on how I might be able to improve in that area?"

Again, by requesting specific feedback, you should gain some specific examples and ideas for how to improve.

The bottom line in handling criticism is that a true professional learns how to build a firm foundation out of the bricks that others throw at them. That is what handling criticism effectively can do for you . . . it can help you build a foundation of mutual respect rather than building a barrier for protection . . . and isn't that what being coachable is all about?

PERSONAL APPLICATION IDEAS:

Let me give you eight final application ideas on how you can become more coachable:

 Keep a "ME FILE" with examples of work you are especially proud of, letters of appreciation, and notes of congratulations you receive throughout the years. As a speaker, I love the letters I receive from my clients, but I am most encouraged by the personal notes from attendees about how the material has positively impacted them. Review your ME file when you are feeling down and need an encouraging boost because of others' criticism.

 Ask your boss and others for positive feedback where none may be offered. An example might be, "What did you especially like about how I handled the project meeting?" Bosses typically only see about 16% of the really terrific things we do. One way to beat the odds is to ask them to look at what we're doing right. The same is true at home. If you desire more positive feedback at home, ask for it. This may seem pretty basic, but I think it comes down to prompting others to give us the kind of feedback we desire and need.

 If you want more positive feedback at home, encourage it. Even though I'm NOT a gourmet cook (nor even do I come close to being a really good cook), that doesn't mean I don't like positive feedback when I've spent time cooking a meal for my husband and sons. Therefore, I've trained the boys since they were able to talk to say, "Good meal, Mom!" Of course, I had to train Jim first. Since we started our boys early, they have gained good habits in praising others. This pays big dividends in creating a positive home environment.

Seek feedback on projects or assignments before a potential miscommunication can occur and mistakes become a crisis. If you are not clear about what your supervisor wants from you, ask, ask, ask! Today's organizations do not have the time or resources for miscommunications. "Better late than never" is not a good motto for today's professionals.

 Do not passively accept criticism or become a silent victim. You will appear to have little self-confidence and may lose the respect of others and yourself.

 Listen carefully to your critic to make sure you understand the criticism.

 Evaluate the source of criticism and whether it was offered constructively, i.e., gives you action to consider and is future-oriented; or destructively, i.e., used words such as "always, never, should" and is focused on the past.

 Don't make globally negative assessments about your character or ability based on one mistake, e.g., "I'm such a jerk! I'll never be any good at this." Give yourself credit for past victories and accomplishments. Being coachable doesn't mean you need to beat up on yourself.

 Lower your emotional temperature and use positive self-talk when dealing with criticism, such as, "I'm OK. I may have made a mistake, but learning from this error will increase my professionalism." See Chapter 10 for more ideas on this topic.

AN EYE FOR AN EYE AND A TOOTH FOR A TOOTH CAN LEAVE YOU BLIND AND TOOTHLESS

"I find it very hard to 'move on' when someone wrongs me in my job. I keep reliving their comments to me and try to figure out why it happened. It makes it difficult for me to treat them well in future interactions. Is it just me or are others this sensitive?"

Assistant Vice President

You know the sage advice, "Never do business with friends." Well, I've written two books on communication skills, so if anyone could do business with friends, I decided it was my husband and me. Or at least that's what I thought. We decided to buy a cottage and ski boat and all the trappings that go with a vacation property with another couple who were our friends. We were living the American dream! But after three years, the American dream died. It just didn't work out. If you are married or in a significant relationship, you know how much work marriage is — well worth the time and effort, but nonetheless still work. In a partnership with another couple, it's basically like being married to two additional people. There was a lot of stress and tension; after three years, we decided to end the partnership.

My husband and I made our decision in February but didn't call

Mike, our partner, until April 15. Mike is a Certified Public Accountant, and we didn't want to stress him in the middle of "tax season." Mike didn't want to let us out of the agreement. We told him he could find another partner or buy us out of the partnership. Mike wavered and stalled and stalled some more. Meanwhile, we had the vacation property and other assets assessed. When we gave Mike the assessment, he told us that the property and assets had depreciated more than that, and the property and assets weren't worth that much money. I felt he was cheating us out of our due money. My husband Jim wisely concluded that we would either fight for the money up-front and then spend it on psychological counseling or take the lower price and cut our losses. I was seething.

As time passed, I got more angry and bitter toward Mike. I thought, "He's stalling this process on purpose just to spite us." It literally took Mike until November to make a decision to buy us out. I was so angry and so hateful toward them. Every time I saw Mike and his wife, which was several times a month, I'd think, "I want them to suffer as much as they made us suffer." I wanted revenge.

Let me tell you what revenge is not. It isn't so overt that I slit their car tires. It wasn't like I was really, truly trying to get revenge. But I kept on reliving our past conversations and past hurt. I gave them the cold shoulder. I wanted them to lose money in their business like we did in our dealings with them. I wanted them to pay the emotional price that I had paid.

> Without forgiveness, resentment builds in us, a resentment which turns into hostility and anger. Hatred eats away at our well-being...therefore forgiveness is an absoljute necessity for continued human existence.
>
> Desmond Tutu

I hate to admit it, but it took me six years to realize that I was the prisoner in this relationship, not Mike nor his wife. Mike had no idea I felt this way. He probably felt my cold shoulder a little bit, but it wasn't like he was hurting inside. In my bitterness, I also concluded wrongly that all personal relationships end like ours did with Mike. I avoided developing deep friendships with other couples for fear I would be hurt again. I would not allow this to happen to me a second time.

The same is true with organizational change. If we are going to heal the pain of change, we must work through this issue of forgiveness. Many times we will not move into the future because somebody in our organization wronged us in the past. Some manager or co-worker did something to us, and we have never moved on. Like me with Mike, we refuse to let go. The result of not forgiving others is that we stay stuck in a painful past.

You might recall a person who wronged you, yet they don't even know they offended you. Inside you're seething. Every time you see them, you're angry and bitter. You wish them the worst. "I hope that something terrible happens to them. I hope they lose their job." It's called revenge. The horrible thing is that revenge usually only hurts the person seeking revenge. In many cases, the other person doesn't even recall the event.

A personal key to healing and moving into the future is healing the past. When someone or an organization has hurt us, our anger over this situation or toward this person often dissolves into a kind of hatred. Why did that person do this to me? They really wronged me. How could the company do that to me? We feel the pain of organizational change. With these hurts and pain, we have two ways we can deal with it: (1) we can forgive those wrongs which will allow us to heal our past. As a result, we can move into the future. Or, (2) we can seek revenge against those who wrong us, but we become bitter in the process. This choice keeps us stuck reliving a past we'd rather forget.

Let's examine a typical organizational change example. Carol is the director of your department, and she is in charge of a reorganization and the combining of two departments due to a corporate merger. There is a supervisory position which is open. You apply for the position, as do several other employees. You have the most seniority in your current department, and people assume you will get the position.

> We can seek revenge against those who wrong us, but we become bitter in the process. This choice keeps us stuck reliving a past we'd rather forget.

Carol calls a meeting to announce the new organizational structure. To your shock and amazement, you have not been selected as the supervisor. Carol introduces the new supervisor to the group — who is from the other organization with which you merged. People all look at you. How will you handle this? You are humiliated. After all you have done for the organization, look how they reward you.

You decided to turn your hurt and hate into revenge. You're going to get even with Carol. You want her to feel as miserable as you do. Every time Carol has contact with you or you see her name, you "see red." You relive the humiliation of that meeting with everyone looking at you to see your reaction.

> Bitterness is a lot like a match: it only burns the person holding on to it.

Revenge is subtly played out in organizations daily. Carol needs information from you. You take your time getting the data to her. Even though you know what she needs and wants, you give her only *exactly* the information she requested. The report she writes is incomplete. She must come back to you for additional statistics. You also find yourself cooperating minimally with other aspects of the reorganization that Carol oversees.

This vengefulness creeps into other aspects of your job. You make the leap and assume that all directors and managers are just

The past can continue to hurt you only if you continue to hold on to it.

like Carol — unfair and unpredictable. When they call, you react the same way to them as you do to Carol. You begin to dislike them. Then, you begin hating your job. It all began with someone inadvertently hurting you. You end up bitter. What we must realize is that bitterness is a lot like a match: it only burns the person holding on to it.

OUR CHOICES

If we want to focus on today and live forward toward the future, we need to learn to forgive those past wrongs and heal our pain. One concept that you might find helpful in forgiving is the idea of empathizing with the person who did us harm. Understanding the person's past history is helpful in gaining perspective on why they did what they did.

I understand now that Mike was looking out solely for his family's interest in giving us less money for the property than was assessed and taking his time to make a decision. I can't blame him for that. Realistically, I was only concerned about my family situation. In Carol's case, perhaps naming a person from the other organization was going to be critical in order to gain cooperation from other departments. Often, we will never know "why" someone makes a decision or says certain things to us. It may help to remember the many times that other people have forgiven you. Think back to your own feelings of gratefulness and relief in situations where you were forgiven.

> (In forgiveness) the operative words are give and gift. You are giving a gift of acceptance to someone, whether that person deserves it or not.
> Joan Borysenko

Robert Enright, Ph.D., of the International Forgiveness Institute, points out several paradoxes that we must come to terms with: You have every right to keep your resentment, but you choose to relinquish it. The offender has no right to your friendliness, yet s/he gets it. The offender is not healed by your forgiveness, yet you are.

Too often we waste time waiting for an apology that never comes or dwell on our victimization. Forgiveness has very little to do with the person who wronged us and everything to do with us and our personal well-being. We need to admit that a wrong was done to us and set our goal on repair- ing the wrong. Forgiveness is a gift that breaks the chains of bitterness and hatred. It is a gift we can consider offering to others through reconciliation.

There are four options for you to consider when forgiving: (1) Stuff It, (2) Spew It Out, (3) Say What You Think, or (4) Silently Forgive.

> *Forgiveness heals, and it may be the cornerstone of maturity and wisdom. All of us receive wounds we don't deserve, and our task as human beings is to transcend them.*
> Roberta Pollack Seid, Ph.D.

STUFF IT

We pay a heavy physical price for a lack of forgiveness in our life. Studies show that hanging on to anger and resentment increases your chance of a heart attack fivefold. It also increases your risk of cancer, high blood pressure, high cholesterol, and a host of other chronic illnesses. Richard Fitzgibbons, M.D., a psychiatrist, concludes that negative feelings can trigger a cascade of stress hormones that accelerates your heart rate, shuts down your immune system, and encourages blood clotting. All of these can lead to heart attacks and strokes. Is that a price worth paying?

Most people who hate someone also hate themselves. When you stuff it, you think of the offender constantly. You have become a prisoner in a torture chamber of your own making. Hate ends up consuming us, not the hated one.

Forgiveness short-circuits the build-up of stress hormones entirely. Forgiveness fosters healthful changes in both your attitude and your body as it lowers your blood pressure and heart rate.

SPEW IT OUT

Spewing out anger or retaliating against the offender is our natural instinctive reaction to being hurt. The fighter in each of us comes out — we want to hurt the person who hurt us. Spewing out angry words never solves a relationship problem — it usually compounds it. Forgiveness does not in any way condone, tolerate, or justify the harmful actions. It does break the grip that past wrong and past pain has on us while freeing us for our future.

When we retaliate, we become bitter and end up getting stuck in the past. We can't move into the future because we keep reliving the past. Lewis Smedes, in his book *Forgive and Forget: Healing the Hurts We Don't Deserve*, says, "Vengeance mires people in a painful and unjust past. They ought to move toward a new future of fairer relationships, but the inner lust for revenge pushes them deeper into the endless repetition of the old unfairness." Keep in mind, it is okay to have anger. We cannot erase the past. We can only heal the pain the past has left behind. Forgiving is anger without hate. It is the only door which can open us up to future possibilities.

> Forgiveness is simply an act of the heart, a movement to let go of the pain, the resentment, the outrage that you have carried as a burden for so long. It is an easing of your own heart...
>
> Jack Kornfield

SAY WHAT YOU THINK WITH LOVE

You can choose to reconcile with the offending person. In effect, you would be saying, "I forgive you, Carol, for not choosing me as the supervisor." The problem with confronting a person with a past hurt is that they have a different perspective about the same situation. Carol believes she selected the best person. Where does your proclamation of forgiveness put you? Later, in Chapter 6, I'll give you a technique for whining with purpose, or telling the truth with love, that may be a better alternative than verbally forgiving Carol for a decision she doesn't regret. Please keep in mind that reconciling with the offender is a definite bonus, but it is not necessary to begin the healing process.

When confronting someone, be careful not to just blurt out what you think. True reconciliation is a well-thought-out process. It is an act of forgiving the offender in order to reestablish the relationship. It is done out of love. You will not have true reconciliation unless a wrong is admitted by the offender, and she or he acknowledges your forgiveness. You must ask yourself in your situation — is this probable?

In my situation with Mike, it had been six years since the incident. To bring up the situation and the things that were done and said didn't make sense. Mike did what he did to protect his family's interest. I didn't expect that he would admit that a wrong was done.

Therefore, reconciliation wasn't a reasonable option. Silently forgiving Mike made the most sense to me. With time, most wounds do heal.

Here are some steps and words you might consider using: 1. Describe the hurtful behavior: *"When you . . . "* 2. Acknowledge your feelings: *"I felt . . . "* 3. Grant forgiveness: *"I want to let you know I forgive you for . . . "* 4. Share your desire to move forward: *"And, I'd like to put this behind us and move on . . . "* 5. *Optional:* Ask for forgiveness for letting your negative feelings persist: "I'd like to ask your forgiveness for being (your feelings) . . . "

SILENTLY FORGIVE

Many times, with forgiveness, silence is golden. For my situation with Mike, I just forgave him silently. When I see him now and talk to him, I can honestly say I wish him well. I even invited him and his wife to a party I recently hosted. Will I ever forget what happened with the partnership? No. Will I ever do business with Mike again? No. Will I ever do business with friends again? Probably not. Although I'm not going to forget what happened, I'm also not going to stay stuck in the past. We must accept personal responsibility for our own future.

> *Power and control is in the pardon, not the killing.*
>
>   *from Schindler's List*

John MacArthur, author of *The Freedom and Power of Forgiveness*, states that silent forgiveness is best used with petty and unintentional offenses. We choose to set aside the wrong and not permit that situation to come between us or foster bitterness in us. If we truly forgive someone, we must resolve not to remember, refuse to hold a grudge, relinquish any claim on recompense, and resist the temptation to brood or retaliate against the offender. We simply bear the insult.

What does MacArthur mean by "resolve not to remember"? Forgiveness doesn't make you lose your memory. It merely takes the sting out of it. Remembering an offense doesn't mean you haven't forgiven the person, and it certainly doesn't disqualify the hard work in moving forward that you have done in your difficult situation. We just need to resolve to not remember our feelings of injustice when they creep back into our memory from time to time.

If this concept of resolving not to remember or "forgive and for-get" is bothersome to you, make your silent forgiveness more tan-gible. Some people find it helpful to write out the situation and then burn or bury the piece of paper it is written on. Others try sitting in one chair with an empty chair facing them. They tell the empty chair what they would like to tell the person who wronged them. You may find it helpful to write a certificate of forgiveness stating that you have, as of today, forgiven. Just know that "for-give and forget" is much easier said than done.

> *I cannot change yester-day. I can only make the most of today, and look with hope towards tomorrow.*
>
> *. Anonymous*

ADMITTING OUR WRONGS

Sometimes forgiveness has more to do with us asking for for-giveness than seeking it. Perhaps someone at your work has become bitter over something you said or did. Often we do things inadver-tently without realizing the cost we will pay in our relationships.

In high school, I didn't fit in and never had a best friend, so I never really learned how to fully appreciate the friend I had in Anne. She and I were very different. Anne was a mother of three preschoolers. They lived on a farm. I was a married career woman who lived in the suburbs. Yet, there was an almost instant chemistry between the two of us. She was the friend I had always dreamed of and never had.

We did what most friends do. We spent hours and hours talking and sharing frustrations and dreams. We grew to love each other more and more as time went on. Then I did the unforgivable. To this day, I'm not sure why I did what I did. I told somebody something Anne had shared with me in confidence.

Even after many tears and asking for forgiveness, the friendship was irrevocably broken. I had always dreamed that Anne would be there with Jim and me for the birth of our children. I had hoped she would be the first person to read the manuscripts for my books — that she would be my biggest cheerleader. But I threw it all away like a cheap, dirty rag without realizing how much of a void the loss of her friendship would leave in my heart.

Five years passed since the incident. A week didn't go by that I didn't think of Anne and pray for her. I kept thinking of how important she was to who I was becoming and that I really should write her and tell her that.

Isn't it true...how quickly we can hurt someone and then just walk away pretending that it didn't really matter in the first place. It matters when someone is hurt. Relationships matter even more. When there is someone in our life we haven't reconciled with, the pain clearly remains, no matter how deeply we bury it. For five years, I grieved over the loss of my friendship with Anne. I thought there wasn't anything more I could do.

Then I decided to write Anne a letter. It went something like this... *"Dear Anne, I meant to write this letter a long time ago. I don't expect this letter to restore our friendship but I wanted you to know the impact of your friendship on my life. You have contributed more than you'll ever know to who I am today. You believed in me when I didn't believe in myself. You thought I was a great speaker before I really became a professional speaker. You always wanted the very best for me in all aspects of my life...Thank you for your gift of friendship and love."*

I wish I could tell you that my friendship with Anne was restored. But life is not always a fairy tale; it doesn't always give us what we desire or hope for. However, one of the keys to personal empowerment is to reconcile our past and tell others what you need to tell them...regardless of the outcome. Who do you need to go to and ask for forgiveness? What has been on your mind, but you have not taken action on it? Do it now. Not tomorrow. Today.

When we are protective, indifferent, and tight-lipped with past unresolved issues, we will experience a lot of sadness in our life. When we give ourselves permission to ask forgiveness, show an interest in others, and tell people the truth with love, we will experience more peace and fulfillment. Our daily challenge is to live our life without regrets.

BENEFITS TO FORGIVENESS

Researchers have found that forgiving results in better sleep, increased feelings of love, an enhanced ability to trust, and an end to the physical symptoms and illness caused by anger. It even lessens the impact of mental illnesses such as depression. Joan Borysenko, a cancer cell biologist and a pioneer in studying how emotions affect the body, believes that forgiveness is the mind's most powerful healing tool.

> I can feel guilty about the past, apprehensive about the future, but only in the present can I act. The ability to be in the present moment is a major component of mental wellness.
>
> Abraham Maslow

Is there somebody you need to forgive in your company who wronged you, who made a bad decision, overlooked you, said something negative? Please realize that when you don't forgive someone it hurts you more than it hurts them. Forgiveness has very little to do with the Mikes and Carols in our lives. It has everything to do with us. And it has everything to do with our ability to move on toward our own future.

Lewis Smedes says this about the healing aspect of forgiveness: "When you forgive someone for hurting you, you perform spiritual surgery inside your soul. You literally cut away the wrong that was done to you so you can see your 'enemy' through the magic eyes (of forgiveness) that can heal your soul."

Realize that the past no longer needs to hold you captive. It can only continue to hurt you if you continue to hold on to it. Let go of it! Give yourself the gift of forgiveness. The very word forgiveness is built around the word "give." There are many people today in organizations who need to give the gift of healing through the power of forgiveness . . . are you one of them?

Personal Application Ideas:

 Make a list of what/who you need to forgive. Note what you felt and what was done.

 Acknowledge your role in the situation. What can you do to prevent the situation from happening in the future (lessons learned)?

 Choose to forgive the person. What method will you use: Silence or Reconciliation?

 To whom do you need to go and ask for forgiveness? What has been on your mind, but you have not taken action on it? Do it!

WHINING
WITH PURPOSE

"Professional staff are worried about career opportunities and their ideas and contributions noted and treated with respect. People at all levels want to be more involved and solving problems."

Quality Manager

I learned some of my lessons about criticism from my mother. Many of our conflicts date back to my grade school days. Even after earning a master's degree and going to work as a trainer in a manufacturing company, our arguments continued. One day I decided to practice what I preached at work. If I was training others how to resolve conflict and to be more assertive, I had better be willing to do the same. After much thought and prayer, I decided to face my mother directly rather than psychoanalyzing every conversation we had.

While spending a weekend with my mom and dad, my husband Jim and I sat down with my parents for about two hours to iron out our past differences. Many tears were shed. As a result of our conversation, I made a compromise: to phone my parents every other Sunday.

Several months later, I called my parents on a Monday since I had attended a business seminar on self-esteem over the weekend. My father is a minister, and my parents had raised me with strict views on Sunday observance, including no eating out, swimming or sports activities, and especially no work of any sort. However, this particular weekend was unusual in that I made the decision to attend this seminar instead of my normal Sunday routine of praise and worship.

Prior to each phone call to my parents, I would have a little pep talk with myself and say, "OK, let's be positive. Let's be assertive. Let's call Mom." When I called my parents that Monday, Jim happened to mention my seminar attendance that weekend, and my mother angrily said, *"What?* You conducted business on Sunday? I can't believe you would do that." Dead silence. I was stunned and angry...who was my mother to judge whether or not I was wrong in attending the seminar? All of my training and the emotional high from the weekend flew out the window. Although very angry, I matter-of-factly replied, "Mother, I don't think you should judge whether or not I should attend the seminar without knowing the content."

More silence. What was I really saying to my mother? Even though it sounded fairly assertive, my tone of voice implied "none of your business." The conversation ended a minute later.

I was devastated. Here we had worked so hard to establish a good relationship, and in a matter of minutes it had been demolished. I had two choices: (1) I could wait for my mom to call and apologize for judging me so quickly, or (2) I could call her up and confront her with how I felt about her comment and what I would instead prefer she do in the future. In other words, whine about her behavior, but do so with a purpose.

It took me three days to calm down enough before I phoned. I wrote notes of what I was going to say and practiced and received feedback from Jim.

This is what happened . . .

"Hi, Mom, this is Patti."

"Hi, Patti."

"Mom, I just wanted to apologize for the way I reacted to you on Monday. May I share with you how I felt about what happened?"

Now, my mom could have said, "I got your apology. That's all I wanted." However, by starting the conversation with an apology and admitting that I was at fault as well, I lessened the potential for defensiveness. Mom replied, "Of course." It's also important to note that I did not apologize for attending the seminar. I merely apologized for my defensive reaction to my mom's statement.

I continued, "Mom, when you criticized me for attending the

seminar over the weekend, I felt hurt that you didn't trust my judgment. In the future, what I would prefer is that you ask me what the seminar was about and why I chose to attend it on a Sunday. This seminar really had an impact on me, Mom, and I hope that I can sit down with you sometime and share what I learned about myself and our relationship. I love you and don't want something like this to come between us."

I'll never forget her reaction. "I know, Patti. I cried for two hours after you hung up. But I never could have called you to apologize."

I learned a great lesson from that incident — sometimes we become the parents and our parents become the children. Sometimes we become the boss or more experienced worker and the boss and experienced worker becomes the "underling." When we know and use the skills of whining with purpose or telling the truth in love, the world becomes ours.

"I wish that I were asked about my "ideas." I'd like to be able to speak freely on these "ideas" without being accused of having a negative attitude or being afraid of change. I want to have more input on matters that are going to affect my working environment."

Attorney

WHINING WITH PURPOSE

So, why do I call giving constructive criticism "whining with purpose"? Because you more than likely will want to criticize when you are in the **Feeling the Pain** phase in the Cycle of Resistance (Chapter 1). When you are in serious pain, you will have to stop yourself from fruitless whining.

Great Spirit, grant that I may not criticize my neighbor until I have walked a mile in his moccasins.

Indian Prayer

Whining with NO purpose will just cause someone to say, "Stop whining and get on board with these changes!" Then, more than likely you will fall prey to the cat reactions discussed in Chapter 2. A typical cat reaction is to "whine and dine" with anyone who will listen (usually someone else who is disgruntled or in pain over the changes).

It's important to realize that many people will think that you're

One of the most important skills we need to develop is the ability to give constructive feedback or to be able to "whine with purpose" to our boss.

just whining or complaining when really you are simply trying to offer constructive criticism. Truly effective team members must learn how to be honest with each other. One of the most difficult things to do in life is to tell the truth in love, particularly when that person is your boss. Yet, one of the most important skills we need to develop is the ability to give constructive feedback or to be able to "whine with purpose."

Many people do not feel comfortable giving criticism to others and as a result do so infrequently. Research on motivation concludes that feedback is one of the biggest motivators for change. Most people are starving for feedback — both positive and negative. Even the people running your organization.

Daniel Webster once said, "There is nothing so powerful as the truth and often nothing as strange." The reality is that we don't necessarily like the truth. It can make us squirm.

🌀 *"We are invited to give suggestions in a cursory way. My sense is that the plan was already in the making and we would help fine tune it. It is a manageable juggling act now that will become a stress-filled nightmare with conflicts of emergency/ crisis versus deadlines for paperwork if we don't have a chance to give input. I see many talented co-workers and myself treated as persons who should just follow directives and not question or give input. Give employees a chance to give input, to shape the change — we want ownership."*

Case Worker

THE COSTS OF NOT WHINING

Even if the leaders in your organization prefer not to hear your feedback, ignoring problematic situations is inappropriate. Most problems do not go away on their own. In fact, not giving critical feedback at appropriate times can cause many change initiatives to fail. In his book for managers, *Beyond the Wall of Resistance,* author Rick Maurer lists these facts . . .

> The truth which makes people free is for the most part the truth which people prefer not to hear.
>
> Herbert Agar

- Across the Board Research study in April 1992 found that Senior Executives in Fortune 500 companies stated that less than half of changes in their organization were successful and that resistance was the main reason for failure. Would "whining with purpose" rather than underground resistance have saved these change initiatives?

- Zinger Miller (1994) determined that more than half of all quality improvement initiatives fail due to resistance. How many organizations failed along with their quality initiatives — perhaps honest feedback would've made a difference?

- In 1995, Application Development Trends found that development of software applications within companies enjoys a very small chance of success: 28% of these projects succeed in small companies, 16% in medium-sized organizations, and only 9% in large companies. Instead of fighting technology changes, why not give purposeful feedback that would enhance the chances for success?

A benefit to giving criticism is that it uncovers problems early on and is the first step to solving them. In the long run, it saves time. Without criticism, minor problems go unsolved and often become major crises. Major crises can even cause an organization to fail. Criticism encourages both the critic and the one criticized to learn and grow, if it's correctly handled.

GUIDELINES ON GIVING CONSTRUCTIVE CRITICISM

Before I give you specific steps on how to whine with purpose, let me give you some general guidelines on giving constructive criticism:

- Focus on the problematic behavior rather than the personality of the person you are criticizing. Be descriptive — not judgmental. Take into account the needs and feelings of the receiver. Is the receiver ready to deal productively with the feedback?

- Always be specific rather than general. Instead of saying, "I feel that you don't really listen to me," say, "You asked for input on project X, and I provided it last Tuesday. I just finished reading your report, and I don't see where you incorporated any of my feedback." People completely miss your point when you aren't specific. If you're going to go to all the bother of giving constructive criticism, don't wimp out on the details.

- Give feedback only on behavior that can be modified. If you criticize my height, there's not much that I can do to change the fact that I'm six feet tall.

- Timing is important. Give the feedback as close as possible to the observed behavior. If you wait too long, the other person might not recall what you are talking about. Your criticism may also be irrelevant at that point.

- It is critical for you to "walk your talk." In other words, if you are going to give a co- worker some feedback on how their being late is causing problems with scheduling work for the department, yet you are consistently late or have an absenteeism problem, they won't take your criticism seriously. Why should they? You lack credibility on that issue.

- Finally, always tell the truth (or give criticism) with love. This is probably the most difficult aspect of truth-telling. A great example is children — they tell the truth, plain and simple, but it isn't told with love — it's just told. This will backfire with adults. If we love or care about someone, we must think before we speak. If we care for our organization or want to continue working for it, we had better think and carefully plan how we are going to tell our truth.

Simply taking the time to plan the constructive criticism can make all the difference in how it will be received and whether or not any changes will take place as a result.

> "I live by a philosophy: Either you adapt to change, or you leave your job. I choose to adapt. Complaining is not an option."
>
> Word Processor

THE DASS SCRIPT

How do you tell your boss that the strategy she or he has selected isn't working or that a particular behavior of theirs is causing a problem for you? Here's how to whine with purpose. I suggest using the **DASS Script.** This is how it works.

Prior to using the DASS Script: Ask for permission. Since your boss has ultimate authority over your pay and promotion, you will want to be very careful about how you give feedback. Before plunging into the **DASS Script,** you will want to ask permission. You may want to begin by saying something like . . . *"Jack, I have an idea that I think may help us work more effectively as a team. Do you have some time this afternoon when we could discuss this?"*

Step one: Describe your boss's problematic behavior. You need to be very specific in your description of your boss's problematic behavior. Do this by giving a recent and specific example. Let's say your boss calls you into his office for a discussion and then promptly begins answering the phone each time it rings (this seems to be a common complaint of employees!). You may want to start out by saying, *"Jack, yesterday when you called me into your office at 3:00 to discuss project X, we were interrupted by four phone calls during our half-hour meeting..."*

Step two: Acknowledge your feelings and the impact on the team. It is important to share your feelings about the situation because it personalizes your criticism. It is impossible for another person to invalidate your feelings because they are just that — your feelings. I'm reminded of the times when I got into trouble with my parents when I was a teenager. I recall preferring any punishment to my parents' saying they were "disappointed" in my behavior. With a punishment, I could complain about my parents and their behavior. However, their "disappointment" caused me to think about my own behavior. Feelings are very powerful and can make a significant difference in how criticism is taken. This is true not only in personal situations but at work as well. No one can question your feelings.

Let's continue with Jack's problematic behavior. (Describe) *"Jack, yesterday when you called me into your office at 3:00 to discuss project X, we were interrupted by four phone calls during our half-hour meeting . . . (Acknowledge) I feel really frustrated (watch your tone of voice) because I know we could have finished our discussion in about 10 minutes if our time wasn't interrupted. Instead, it took 30 minutes to deal with my questions . . . "*

If you stop after step two, I consider this "whining." You're just complaining to your boss about his irritating behavior. You are venting and getting it off your chest, but that's it. Instead, whine *with purpose.* That is, move immediately to steps four and five, which are focused on *solving* the problem. Don't resort to "bitchin," instead "pitch in" by giving your boss a potential solution.

Step three: Specify a Solution. Tell your boss what alternative behavior you would prefer. Provide an action plan and solution to the problem. Back to Jack: (Describe) *"Jack, yesterday when you called me into your office at 3:00 to discuss project X, we were interrupted by four phone calls during our half-hour meeting . . . (Acknowledge) I feel really frustrated because I know we*

> We must dare to think 'unthinkable' thoughts. We must learn to explore all the options and possibilities that confront us in a complex and rapidly changing world. We must learn to welcome and not to fear the voices of dissent. We must dare to think about the 'unthinkable things' because when things become unthinkable, thinking stops and action becomes mindless.
>
> James W. Fulbright

could have finished our discussion in about 10 minutes if our time wasn't interrupted. Instead, I had to take 30 minutes of your time to deal with my questions... (Specify a Solution) *What I'm wondering is whether you would be willing to hold your phone calls when we meet. Is that a possibility?..."*

Step four: Show *How the Team Benefits.* This is the final and most important step. Envision everyone (your boss, employees, co-workers, children) all walking around with the following stamped on their head: **WIIFM? What's in it for me?** Your boss will not be motivated to change his or her behavior unless they will benefit.

Let's conclude the example with Jack: (Describe problem) *"Jack, yesterday when you called me into your office at 3:00 to discuss project X, we were interrupted by four phone calls during our half-hour meeting . . .* (Acknowledge feelings) *I feel really frustrated because I know we could have finished our discussion in about 10 minutes if our time wasn't interrupted. Instead, I had to take 30 minutes of your time to deal with my questions . . .* (Specify a Solution) *What I'm wondering is whether you would be willing to hold your phone calls when we meet. Is that a possibility? ...* (Show benefits) *The real benefit of limiting our interruptions is the time savings. By using voice mail, we'll only need to spend about a third of our time meeting, and I'll be able to get those projects I'm working on for you done on time.* (Wrap-Up) *Would you be willing to try this?"*

Be open to compromise and discussion as Jack considers your ideas.

While you are providing someone your unsolicited feedback, be very aware of your tone of voice and gestures. Don't pout, whine, or sound aggravated — it will only make things worse. Sound genuine and caring. You'll have a much better chance of being heard.

Since many people find the "feeling" part of the technique so difficult, the following list may be helpful in determining how you feel about the problematic behavior at hand.

Vocabulary of Negative Feelings

afraid	devastated	hurt
offended	agitated	discredited
indignant	perturbed	annoyed
disgusted	inferior	put down
anxious	dismayed	insignificant
put off	apprehensive	distressed
intimidated	puzzled	ashamed
down	inadequate	neglected
belittled	embarrassed	irked
rejected	bewildered	enraged
irritated	resentful	bitter
exasperated	left out	seething
bothered	exploited	let down
troubled	burned up	furious
lonely	turned off	confused
helpless	mad	uptight
disappointed	hostile	outraged
unsure	discouraged	humiliated
overlooked	upset	

Following are several versions to try with a co-worker. See if you can pick out the most effective example.

You and your co-worker Michael work as technicians in the engineering lab. You are working on a major product redesign for a customer. You provide him with the rough draft of the technical changes that are necessary to make, which he in turn enters into the computer system. A small problem has developed, however: Michael consistently forgets to return your draft copy when giving you the final design printout. Here are three different ways of reacting to this problem. You could say to him . . .

Option 1

"Michael, you can't expect me to remember all the changes I asked you to make. I need you to return the draft copy with the completed work."

Option 2

"Michael, if you would do what you are supposed to do, I would-

*n't have to bug you every 10 min-
utes for my draft copy. How many
times do I have to remind you?"*

Option 3

*"Michael, when you don't return
my draft copy, I have to reproof. I'd
appreciate it if you'd send the draft
copy back to me with the completed
work. This will save both of us
time and enable us to implement
these changes more quickly."*

> Problems are the cut-
> ting edge that distin-
> guishes between success
> and failure. Problems
> call for our courage
> and our wisdom;
> indeed, they create our
> courage and our wis-
> dom.
>
> M. Scott Peck

Option 1 comes across as parental and demanding. When the co-worker attacked Michael, they probably lost his attention because the attack made him feel defensive.

Option 2 is accusatory, whiny, and sarcastic. It utilizes the over-generalization "every" which automatically will flash a red flag for Michael.

Option 3 is the best purposeful statement because it requests a specific behavior and provides a rationale for why the requested behavior is a "win-win" situation for all involved.

Here's a final work scenario.

You are coordinating a change-initiative project with a supervisor from another department. You are frustrated because she doesn't return your phone calls promptly, which is causing delays in the project's implementation deadlines. A whining-blaming statement might be: *"I see now why you can never get anything done. You're too disorganized to even find my phone messages on your desk. No wonder everyone has to call you 2-3 times to get the information they need."*

Instead, try saying . . . *"When you don't return my phone messages, I feel irritated because it delays me on my part of the change project. What I would prefer is if you or one of your staff members would simply give me a phone call and let me know when you can get back to me with the information I need. I'm sure this will help both of us become more effective."*

Finally, how about using this technique at home? Your child does not clean up his or her bedroom as requested. The whining statement is: *"Your room is a disaster zone. You make twice as much work for me. Why don't you ever pick up your bedroom like I ask?"*

It is more purposeful and effective if you say, *"Honey, when you don't pick up your room like I ask you to, I really get annoyed. Let's work out a cleaning schedule that we can both live with so that I don't need to bug you about it any more."*

It is important to note that the **DASS Script** is purposeful, focused, and brief. The intent is not to spark a lengthy discussion. Both people must benefit. If you feel like screaming at the other person, you probably have waited too long. That's why it is important to give constructive criticism as soon as possible after the problem behavior occurs. This allows the conversation to be purposeful rather than blaming or accusatory. Make sure you don't resort to "whining and dining" by spreading rumors and gossip like the cat reactions discussed in Chapter 3.

> ⊚ *"The potential of an uncertain future has increased stress in my life. Rumors, naturally, with accurate and inaccurate information is being passed among all employees. Fears are induced by these rumors."*
>
> *Project Manager*

BECOME PART OF THE SOLUTION, NOT PART OF THE PROBLEM

Another strategy that will help you become part of the solution instead of part of the problem is as follows:

1) **Listen with an open mind to the person's Game Plan.** You may want to say, " *your goal is* (explain in your words your understanding of this person's desired outcome)...*and your strategy for achieving that goal is* (his/her suggested game plan).

2) **Explain your concerns from the playing field.** Then explain why you don't think their plan will work. If at all possible, provide statistics or examples. *"My concern(s) with your strategy is..."*

3) **Provide your suggested solution or other options.** This step is absolutely critical! Give alternative solutions or options that will still meet the person's goals. For example, *"Another way we could still get (their goal)...is...(your idea, solution, or alternative). Will that meet your needs?"*

Most bosses want to achieve an outcome/goal — they are not necessarily stuck on their specific strategy to achieve the goal. Many are willing to listen to other ideas as long as their goals get met. Always go to a boss not only with the problem but with a solution as well.

> *The world is too dangerous for anything but truth, and too small for anything but love.*
> *Rev. William Sloane Coffin*

WHINING IN WRITING

We have covered the basic verbal skills in whining with purpose. However, there is one way to give criticism that has not yet been addressed — how to give written criticism. It should be recognized that it is far better to give criticism in person than by letter/e-mail for several reasons: (1) with writing, you will not be able to discern how the other person is receiving the criticism, (2) you will have to wait for a reply, which can be stressful, and (3) the choice of words becomes even more critical because the receiver will have the opportunity to read and reread your criticism. In verbal criticism, you only give the criticism once and it is over.

Here's a true example of what happened at a university when two highly educated professionals (one a supervisor, the other his subordinate) refused to talk across the cubicle aisle from each other. Neither was willing to quit the e-mail flaming game. See if you can read into their statements and how each person imagined what the other person was "really" saying.

Fr: Jose

To: Susan

Susan,

Unlike other staff members, you have not been turning in sick leave forms the day after returning to work. From now on, please do so — it is university policy to turn in the forms the day after returning. Also, from now on if you need to communicate with me about nontechnical issues, please do so through written message, e-mail, or a meeting with Harry (Jose's boss), per our agreed upon arrangement.

Jose

Susan's reply:

Fr: Susan

To: Jose

Jose,

I do not turn in sick leave forms the day after I have used sick leave because I can often make it up by working additional hours. Also, I understand from Mary that we are expected to turn in sick leave and vacation forms by the end of the month, not the next day.

Susan

To: Susan

From: Jose

Susan,

You need to be consistent with unclassified staff in this office as well as other staff. Please turn in sick leave forms the day after returning to work.

Jose

The end result of this relationship was that when Jose went on sabbatical, Susan took a job elsewhere in the university. The damage was irreversible. The flaming game was only one symptom of an inability and unwillingness to communicate honestly with each other.

Some find giving written criticism easier because there is no immediate interpersonal conflict. The person is unable to respond immediately and spontaneously. However, as a result, the receiver will probably interpret the criticism as much more formal and final when received in that manner. You will need to consider seriously if that is the impression you want to leave. It may be appropriate to send a *follow-up* letter of criticism after you have discussed the problem in person. However, it is best not to substitute a letter for personal contact.

If you do choose to send a letter, keep these points in mind:

(1) Choose your words carefully. You may want to have someone read through the letter/e-mail before you send it. Don't

let anger seep into the content. Tone comes across more strongly when written.

(2) Use a positive tone when stating the reason why you want to solve the problem.

(3) Include specific examples of the problematic behavior.

(4) Suggest that the other person think over the situation and how it can be resolved. Indicate when you will be calling to follow up on the feedback so the two of you can resolve the problem.

(5) Include positive statements in the conclusion of the letter as to why you believe this will not continue to be a problem and reaffirm the worth of the other person.

WHEN NOT TO WHINE

Keep in mind that there will be times when you will not want to give criticism.

- Do not give criticism when you are angry, stressed, or testy.

- Do not give criticism when the timing is bad or when the person receiving the criticism cannot take action on it.

- Do not give criticism when you do not have specific facts or evidence to back up your feedback.

- Do not give criticism as a power play — to lower the esteem of the other or to make yourself appear self-important.

- Do not expect to see results from your criticism if you have not set up mutual goals or expectations prior to the situation's occurring.

Providing others with honest feedback in the form of criticism, or whining with purpose, can deepen our interpersonal relationships with them and can provide us — and them — with the tools necessary to

There is a right time for everything...
A time to kill, a time to heal;
A time to destroy, a time to rebuild;
A time to cry, a time to laugh;
A time to tear, a time to repair;
A time to be quiet, a time to speak up.
Ecclesiastes 3: 3-7

improve productivity and self-esteem. My conversation with my mom helped to deepen and mature our relationship as mother and adult daughter.

The bottom line is this: Become part of the solution and not part of the problem by sharing your truth in love. Samuel Butler once said, "If people would dare to speak to one another unreservedly, there would be a good deal less sorrow in the world a hundred years hence." He is right. Let's change our world!

Personal Application Ideas:

 About what have I been whining?

 In what current situation can I constructively and purposefully give criticism? With whom should I share my criticism?

 In what specific ways do I plan to become part of the solution rather than part of the problem?

PART III:

OVERCOMING THE PERSONAL 'NOTS' THAT KEEP US IN OUR RESISTANCE TO CHANGE

WHEN YOU'RE AT THE END OF YOUR ROPE, LET GO!

"I am concerned that I will face rapid burnout and loss of efficiency because of the high levels of frustration with my job. The frustration often comes from having too many demands placed on us that don't seem relevant to our goals. When can I do my real job? While we all know that "change can be good" and it offers "opportunities for growth," too much change which is implemented too rapidly and too persistently creates a sense that one is never competent doing one's job because you never reach the point on the learning curve where you can achieve maximum efficiency and productivity."

Early Intervention Specialist

Several years ago, I went on a weekend spiritual retreat. I had avoided going on this retreat for two years. Instinctively I knew I would be challenged about my need for control, so I avoided the inevitable by not going. I entered that retreat thinking to myself, "Patti Hathaway, you have really got yourself together. You have built a successful business. You have a wonderful husband and two adorable sons. You have managed your life well. What if you get challenged on this control issue and let go? What if you let go of managing your life, and you lose everything you have worked so hard to gain? Could you live with yourself if you lost it all?" Those thoughts terrified me. Still I went.

For most of the women on this retreat, it was a positive mountaintop experience. As a result of my faulty thinking, I spent most of the weekend in the valley fighting for control over my soul. Could I give up that control? Near the very end of the weekend, I finally learned how to let go, to let God take over the reigns. It did not come easily or without a lot of personal pain. But what I did experience was a tremendous sense of relief, release, and peace.

TO CONTROL OR NOT TO CONTROL

> 🌸 *"I feel devalued, disregarded, disposable, yet I do support the big picture purpose of the changes. There's no going back, but I mourn what my job used to be. Some days I respond as if abused by my employer. I know that some of these feelings, if not all, are a response to a change I was powerless to stop."*
> *Quality Enhancement Coordinator*

I learned an important lesson that weekend. Giving up control isn't just a one-time event. For each of us in a change situation, dealing with our control needs will be ongoing. Organizational change is about what we control and what we don't control. It is about a struggle every single day to focus on the right things. Each of us can be a winner in change and feel a sense of personal power if we focus on certain things.

> There is only one way to happiness and that is to cease worrying about things which are beyond the power of our will.
>
> Epictetus

There are basically three things we can focus on in change situations: (1) the things we Can Control, (2) the things we May Have Influence over, and (3) the things we Cannot Control.

THE WINNER'S GRID

The Winner's Grid below provides a map for taking more personal power in change situations. There are two ways we choose to act when it comes to the things we **Cannot Control:** (1) **Just do it!** by taking action on those things; OR (2) **Let it go.**

Let's examine the far right quadrant. In change situations, we pri-

	Can Control	May Have Influence	Cannot Control
Just Do It!	**Game Face**	**Cheerleader**	**Hanger-On**
Let Go!	**Armchair Quarterback**	**"Boo" Bird**	**Graceful Exit**

marily tend to focus on the last category: **Cannot Control.** Here are some examples of things that might belong in the Cannot Control category: company profit and loss; the market/economy; policies and procedures; management decisions; staffing levels; our supervisor (although I coauthored a book entitled *Managing Upward* so I disagree with this one); the business plan; time; the future; the weather.

If you are taking action in areas you cannot control, you will feel frustrated and angry and become like the aging athlete or *Hanger-On.* You can gain release and relief if you let go of situations and circumstances over which you have no control. You will experience firsthand the relief of a *Graceful Exit.* I had to learn to take a Graceful Exit at the retreat and let go of the supposed control I had over my life.

When we take action on things we don't control, we become *Hangers-On.* Hanging on is a term used in sports for athletes who hang on beyond the time they really should have retired. It happens not only in sports but even in the workplace. We hang on to old vendettas, hang on to the old way of doing things, hang on to the fact that we cannot control certain things but we sure are going to try. As a result, we become angry, frustrated people. We are angry at the system. We are upset with the organization. We are frustrated with our boss. We're carrying a grudge against our co-worker. We're angry because we've chosen to hang on to things that we have no control over.

We can feel a sense of relief and release if we let go or gracefully exit out of the need we have to control the things that don't belong in our sphere of influence. What does the word "exit" mean?

We hang on to old ways of doing our work. As a result, we become angry, frustrated people.

It doesn't mean to jump the organizational ship, although I think in some cases that may be the best choice if a person cannot let go of the things they don't control. What is meant by *Graceful Exit* is to let go gracefully. To "let go" of the areas over which you have no control.

One of the best examples of a *Graceful Exit* in the sports world is the retirement of basketball star Michael Jordan of the Chicago Bulls. Jordan was still a phenomenal basketball player by anyone's standards when he announced his retirement. He decided he just didn't want to play the game anymore. He "let go" gracefully while he was on top of the game. He didn't wait until people were questioning his talent and ability.

The word "grace" is not used much in our vocabulary. Grace means "reprieve; a temporary exemption." Grace must be given by someone; it

> This is the worst pain a person can suffer: to have insight into much and power over nothing.
> *Herodotus*

cannot be yanked from them. When we take a graceful exit, we voluntarily give up that which we cannot control.

LETTING GO BY STREAMLINING YOUR JOB

"With the growth of the organization and the integration of the departments, we have all had to take on additional work with the same number of hours in a day to perform our tasks. This requires many hours of overtime in order to perform the job in an organized manner."

Software Technician

Often organizational changes bring additional roles and responsibilities. Many times we never take the time to look at what we should let go of from our old job. We need to consider how to streamline our job tasks as a practical way of letting go. Following are some

> The best preparation for tomorrow is to do today's work superbly well.
> Sir William Osler

areas and questions for you to consider and discuss with others in your department.

Bureaucracy Elimination: What unnecessary administrative tasks, approvals, and paperwork could be eliminated?

"Changing demands and unexpected deadlines pull the group in differing directions. Frustrations of individual requirements break down ability to assist others with their problems. Expanding workload causes pressure and subsequently interpersonal friction. Need to identify old tasks no longer required to provide time to perform new or expanded tasks."

Vice President of Operations

Duplication Elimination: What identical activities are performed in several places or at different points in the process?

Simplification: How could we reduce the complexity of our department's processes or procedures? How could we make our paperwork more uniform?

Standardization: Are there any uniform ways of doing some of our department activities/processes/procedures/paperwork so that we all could do the activity in the same way and save time?

Automation and/or Mechanization: How could we apply tools, technology, equipment, and computers to boring, routine activities to free us to do more creative activities?

> 🌀 *"I'm excited, but things move faster than you can learn everything you need to know. Trying to do your job while expected to learn new stuff is frustrating."*
>
> *Data Processing Coordinator*

Communication: What are the problems with the current means of communication? What solutions could we recommend? How would we like our management team to communicate to us? How would we like to communicate to the managers?

Teamwork: How can our managers be more effective in their jobs and in promoting teamwork? What can we do to be more effective in our jobs and as a team?

A CASE STUDY: SLEEPING WITH THE ENEMY

There is no greater opportunity for graceful exits than in a merger situation. Here is a true case study with specific recommendations that you might find helpful.

> We can easily manage, if we will only take each day, the burden appointed for it. But the load will be too heavy for us if we carry yesterday's burden over again today, and then add the burden of the morrow to the weight before we are required to bear it.
>
> John Newton

SITUATION

In 1991, Dr. William Martin was doing his annual strategic planning session. He interviewed several insurance executives to try to predict what would happen in the marketplace with managed care. He was convinced that insurers would prefer to deal with as few providers as possible. His medical practice would need to become vertically integrated to be successful. After examining several options, he decided to contact the five-office, eight-doctor Kahn & Diehl Centers for Progressive

Eye Care to discuss joining forces. Optometrist and co-owner Paul Kahn would consider it only if the transaction were a merger and they could be equal partners.

After consulting with legal consultants, two professional corporations were developed — one medical and one optometric. Once the merger was consummated, the problems started. Internally, it was a challenge to make diverse backgrounds come together. For instance, the medical side of the business made extensive use of computers and used comprehensive financial controls and management information systems. The optometric practice used 3x5 cards and used a handwritten ledger system. Dr. Martin and Mary Martin, the operations director, pushed the optometric business into modernization and received "tremendous opposition." Some of the employees felt that it was a "hostile takeover" — 30% of the employees gracefully exited.

There was tremendous financial pressure, but the expected surge in med-surgical contracts was slow to come. The practice earned next to nothing the first year of operation. The end result, however, produced several key benefits: *surgical volume* increased and was profitable from the first year of operation. The practice as a whole last year also posted a profit. *Preparedness.* When managed care fully arrives in northwestern Ohio, the practice is well-positioned to bid on contracts. They can offer the whole package or cafeteria-style. *Economies of scale.* The practice has been able to economize on expensive instruments. They have also been able to hire a full-time advertising executive, which would not have been possible with an individual practice. *Patient care.* The merger has increased the technical abilities of the entire practice. Dr. Kahn states, "I see patients I wouldn't have seen before and I've learned to use techs, including scribes. I have learned more in the past two years than I did in the previous 23."

RECOMMENDATIONS

Management Strategies: If you are a manager in a similar merger situation, here are some strategies for you to consider.

1) Share the fiscal books openly with staff so they can see the logic behind the merger and the need to implement new management systems. Employees desperately want to see "what's in it for me?" Ultimately, these changes will pro-

duce increased profitability which in turn may lead to increased salaries.

2) Encourage employee input into changes which directly impact them.

3) Keep staff up to date with managed care happenings so they can see the "bigger picture."

4) Don't just teach technical skills, also explain the "why" and benefits behind the need for modernization.

5) Address rumors as they occur.

6) Praise progress in learning, and celebrate small successes.

7) Hire replacement employees as much for their positive attitude and ability to deal with change as for their technical abilities and expertise.

8) Provide training to help the employees understand the change-management process. Have the training pay particular attention to the challenges of melding of the two cultures.

Employee Strategies: If you are an employee in a similar merger situation, here are some strategies for you to consider.

1) Ask questions of the owners and management. Provide on-going input.

2) Embrace technology and more efficient ways of doing business.

3) Always remember the importance of customer service no matter what is happening within or to the organization.

4) Keep in mind the big picture and the vision for where the organization is going. Take pride in being a pioneer in your field.

5) Look for ways to build a team between offices and locations.

6) Take an interest in cross-training so you can be of assistance to others.

7) Keep healthy and raise your resistance to stress.

8) Minimize, as well as possible, other personal changes in your life.

We need to learn how to *gracefully exit* and let go. In order to move into the future, we need to let go of the past. Perhaps some of us may need to reread Chapter 5 on forgiveness when we think of the *Graceful Exit*? What have you been hanging on to? What is something that you need to gracefully exit out of in your job? You can't move forward into the future if you're still hanging on to the past.

It's like blowing up a balloon and then letting it go. When you release a balloon, you release and relieve the pressure. The same thing can happen at work when we recognize what we don't control and let go of our desire to control it. With organizational change, as with my control concerns at the retreat, it will probably be a daily struggle for us to let go. Our challenge is to "own" and take action only on those things which we can control.

PERSONAL APPLICATION IDEAS:

 What have you been hanging on to that you need to relinquish and let go of?

 Which of the streamlining strategies might help in your job?

BYE-BYE, BOO BIRD

"I feel disempowered, frustrated, and angry. I am confused because no one is up-front about what is going on other than to say that this reorganization is due to a philosophical shift. Philosophy is fine but what about how we implement it? There has been a lack of direction and collaboration about issues that affect all of us. I feel no one hears my voice in regards to our department. The new structure adds more hierarchy and less collaboration, which can be messy yes, but also leads to people not owning and feeling like they are valued members of the community."

Academic Advisor

At the fall parent-teacher conference, my oldest son's third-grade teacher strongly suggested that we get Bryan assessed for learning disabilities. Bryan could read well but comprehended little of what he read. He also struggled with writing. Three months later at the assessment meeting, we learned that Bryan did not have any learning disabilities, but he did have Attention Deficit Disorder (ADD). He had trouble focusing and with controlling his impulsiveness.

Prior to this diagnosis, Jim and I had always jokingly talked about kids with ADD as really having "Discipline Deficit Disorder." Now we had to come to grips with the fact that *our* child had ADD. Suddenly we had to re-examine and change our beliefs and mindset. Through research we learned that Bryan's ADD had little to do with our parenting skills or lack thereof.

As I was driving to Cleveland for a program the day after the diagnosis, I wept. "What are we going to do with Bryan? This is going to make life such a hassle," I thought to myself. My heart broke for my son and the inevitable struggles he would encounter. Yet, I knew I couldn't do anything about it. Coincidentally, the sun was shining in Columbus while there was a huge storm in Cleveland. While I was driving on the freeway, I

> I know God will not give me anything I can't handle. I just wish that He didn't trust me so much.
> Mother Teresa

drove directly into two double rainbows. I knew the rainbows were a gift from God that spoke to my heart and said, "You don't control this situation, Patti, but there's always promise. There is hope for your son. You can be Bryan's biggest cheerleader and make something positive come out of this. Just focus on what you can influence and give the rest to Me." Although there are still many times I'd like to change Bryan, I cannot change who Bryan is. What I must focus on is how I choose to influence him.

THE WINNER'S GRID

The Winner's Grid provides a map for taking more personal power in change situations. There are six ways to act in any situation. We already examined the Cannot Control column in chapter eight. Let's look at the middle column. When you encourage those around you to become Change Agents rather than Change Victims, you will be valued as a **Cheerleader.** The other option is to be a **"Boo Bird"** by just sitting back and letting your opportunity to influence others slip by.

Think about all the things that could be listed under the "May

	Can Control	May Have Influence	Cannot Control
Just Do It!	Game Face	Cheerleader	Hanger-On
Let Go!	Armchair Quarterback	"Boo" Bird	Graceful Exit

Have Influence" category, including: others' attitudes and/or ways of thinking; quality of product; job productivity; organizational changes; safety; company performance; efficiencies; quality in my department; communication tools; personal safety; some policies and procedures; organizational profit; budget, and so on.

Do you know that by merely walking into work you can influence how the day's going to go for some people? Let's say you had a late reorganization task force meeting and didn't get back before everybody had left for the day. The next morning, you are running late. You immediately go to your office without greeting anyone. Before you close your office door, the rumors have already started. "I bet it was a really bad meeting." "He didn't say anything to me this morning. I wonder if he heard we're all getting fired, but he's just not telling us." You haven't said anything. But others interpreted your nonverbal behavior to say, "This is bad. This is terrible." We influence other people's attitudes a great deal by how we act nonverbally. All of us have a choice of whether or not we will become a **cheerleader** or **boo bird** in the areas where we influence others.

BE A CHEERLEADER

A *cheerleader* is both an encourager and an excellent communicator. Very few "cheerleaders" are paid to cheer at a professional sporting event. A cheerleader is not the coach who calls the plays. She or he merely cheers on the people who are playing the game. The same is true in our organizations. Most of us are not the coaches calling the plays in the game of change. Yet if we want our organization to be successful, all of us need to become "cheerleaders" who are committed to communicating continuously. We need to encourage those around us.

A cheerleader often influences the outcome of the game and has an immediate and definite impact on those around them. Here are some specific organizational cheerleader strategies:

- Give input when none is asked for.
- Encourage your co-workers when they are discouraged.
- Volunteer to serve on transition task forces.
- Constantly look for ways to help your team/organization get better at what you do.

AVOID BECOMING A "BOO BIRD"

As a cheerleader, you are an encourager and communicator. You give input and provide options. Unfortunately, some people would rather mutter, "Let the leaders make their own mistakes. They'll come crawling back to us later looking for ideas." The Boo Bird's attitude is "Why bother?" The organizational ship is sinking. What the Boo Bird doesn't realize is that they are on the sinking ship and they will sink with it. When we sit back and just boo, not only does the organization lose, so do we. Even if we don't lose our jobs, others may lose respect for us, and we ultimately lose a lot of respect for ourselves.

I have to admit that when I began doing extensive research on Attention Deficit Disorder — what causes it, strategies for how to deal with it, etc. — it didn't take long for me to surmise that in most cases, ADD is hereditary. We certainly knew immediately who

If we want our organization to be successful, all of us need to become "cheerleaders" who are committed to communicating continuously. We need to encourage those around us.

Bryan did NOT get it from — me! In fact, while I was sharing the descriptive characteristics of ADD with my husband, Jim said to me, "Boy, you know a lot of those characteristics fit for me, too." I lost it! I snapped at Jim and said, "I can't even handle having an ADD child, much less an ADD husband. Don't even go there." Admittedly, a part of me just wanted to give up and become a "Boo Bird."

> ✿ *"There are many unknowns during this transition to the new administration. I have tried to continue work as usual because I do not have any control over these changes. I evaluate the impact of these changes as they are made. Others worry and speculate about future changes, and then worry about their speculations."*
>
> *Assistant Director*

A **Boo Bird** is a person who comes to a professional sporting event. They put a paper bag over their head with holes cut out for the eyes. They wear the paperbag so no one will identify them as a fan of the team. They watch a game and "boo" the entire time. They are only there to bother the players and to discourage the other fans. They are helpless, hopeless people who just boo. One of the best examples is the New Orleans Saints' Boo Birds. They call themselves the "New Orleans' Ain'ts." Boo Birds do obnoxious things like having a big sign that says, www.bengalsstink.com. Many a game has been won or lost due to the cheerleaders in the crowd. What kind of life is it to put a bag over your head and boo?

How does booing help encourage any organization to succeed? How is our own attitude impacted when we are consistently negative? If your organization is so bad, why do you stay? None of us deserve to be in an organization if we're not willing to get in and put a game face on when life isn't all that pleasant. Keep in mind the Chapter 2 explanation of the fact that we take our reactions and attitudes home with us every night — is that good news for you?

Much of what we do day in and day out influences those around us. Don't give up on your ability to make a difference in your organization! The moment you sit back and become a Boo Bird is the moment you will begin to feel helpless and hopeless. The reality is that you can make a difference in the outcome of organizational change. The truth is that some people don't want to be encouraged or positively influenced by anyone. However, even if you can influence only a small part of the organization, be a cheerleader wherever you can make a difference.

Although there certainly have been times with Bryan that I just wanted to be a Boo Bird and let Jim deal with him, I quickly surmised that putting an ADD dad with an ADD child is a recipe for frustration. I have no control over Bryan nor his ability to learn. I can't go into his class and take the tests for him. The best I can do is influence Bryan and be his *cheerleader.*

What is your chosen role — to be a cheerleader or a boo bird?

	Can Control	**May Have Influence**	**Cannot Control**
Just Do It!	**Game Face**	**Cheerleader**	**Hanger-On**
Let Go!	**Armchair Quarterback**	**"Boo" Bird**	**Graceful Exit**

THE ARMCHAIR QUARTERBACK

If you take action or "Just Do It!" on the things you can control, you will feel good and powerful. You will have conquered the ability to put on a **Game Face.** However, if you choose not to take action on things that you could control, you will feel helpless and hopeless and become an **Armchair Quarterback.**

We've all seen "armchair quarterbacks." They are the people who sit back in an easy chair with the remote control watching football. They moan, "If I were the quarterback, I would have called a different play." Which is why they're sitting in their armchair with a beer? Give me a break. They are not actually practicing hours every day preparing to play. They aren't on the field getting battered and bruised during the game.

It's easy to sit and think to ourselves, "If I were in management, things would be a lot different. If I were a Vice President/Manager (fill in the blank), the change never would have been introduced the way it was. I would have involved the employees. I would have had a heart for the people." If we stay in our armchairs long enough, we can end up "ROTJ" — Retired On The Job. When we criticize the change process and don't get involved, we don't impact the change. It's no more fun to play football from an armchair than it is to "whine and dine" about change to someone who cannot impact the change.

Think about all the things we can control: our attitude; morale by encouraging cooperation and passing on information; rewards; diet, exercise, relaxation; our niceness; showing up for work; providing positive feedback to others; our personal productivity and work habits; what we think about; the skills we implement (mirroring, whining with purpose, etc.); our level of efficiency; our work quality; our communication (up, down, to co-workers); personal safety; budget; and so much more. If you really sat down and brainstormed ideas, you would come up with many more ideas in the Can Control category than in the May Have Influence and Cannot Control categories.

"Our program is constantly changing. I think change is a very good thing. Without it, we would be stuck in the dark ages and the disabled population that we work with would be forever locked behind doors. We must continue to adapt and change to meet the changing needs of the world we live in."

Teacher

THE GAME FACE

We need to learn how to get in the game and take action on the things we can control. One of the best examples of putting on a *Game Face* was the 1997 Super Bowl football game. Most of the pre-game attention was on quarterback John Elway. It was Elway's fourth year to bring the Denver Broncos to the Super Bowl. His team lost the first three times he quarterbacked in the Super Bowl.

The most interesting story behind the 1997 Super Bowl was not Elway but Terrell Davis, the Broncos' running back. Davis was clearly the star of the first quarter of the football game. However, after a brutal tackle, Davis left the game with a migraine headache.

He was out of the game the entire second quarter and the extended half time. Despite his pain, Davis fought back, woozy from the medication, to play the second half of the game brilliantly. Not only did Davis help the Broncos win the 1997 Super Bowl but he was also awarded the most valuable player award.

Personally, I don't think Davis was miraculously healed of his migraine headache during half time. He didn't come back in the second half saying, "I feel great. I love playing football." I think Terrell Davis forced himself to put on a *game face* and said, "I have to just do it. I don't care how much pain I'm in. I don't care how uncomfortable I am. I'm going to go in and play this game because I can." Have you ever suffered from a migraine headache? Did you ever play football with a migraine headache? It's doubtful. Terrell Davis's courageous act exemplifies the term "game face." We can all learn from his example.

A *game face* is what winners put on in changing organizations. Change will be painful. But all of us can put on our game face and just do it. We need to "suck it up" and force ourselves to be productive. We can make our attitude positive because we control it, NOT because we feel like it. If we choose to put a game face on, we'll feel good and powerful, but not necessarily happy. Happiness does not always come hand in hand with feeling good and powerful. Terrell Davis probably felt somewhat powerful while playing in the Super Bowl, but not necessarily happy about his condition. Happiness came with the victory, not during the play.

> *"The length of time it has taken to implement our reorganization has been tremendous and has had more impact than the actual change event! It just seems to drag on and on. Many employees are demotivated by the fact that their old jobs aren't quite finished and their new jobs haven't quite been defined. Many people are in a state of suspended animation."*
>
> *Senior Engineer*

OUR CHOICE

We all have choices. You are going to choose in your change situation to become either a victim of change or a change agent. It is not an easy process. If you go back to your organization with a vision to put your game face on and to be a cheerleader, inevitably

> People are always blaming their circumstances for what they are. I don't believe in circumstances. The people who get on in this world are the people who get up and look for the circumstances they want, and, if they can't find them, make them.
> George Bernard Shaw

you will encounter people in your organization who will not be supportive of that decision. It is difficult to thrive in change when we're in pain. Our negative co-workers will want us to sink low and to feel as lousy about our situation as they do. Yet, the decision is ultimately our own. What will your choice be?

Where do you fit in *The Winner's Grid* model? Are you someone who sticks with it and does what you can when you can, encouraging and cheering people in the process? Do you do what you can? Are you gracefully exiting out of the things you cannot control because that's best for you?

CASE STUDY: IF IT AIN'T BROKE, DON'T FIX IT —DEALING WITH A REORGANIZATION

There is no greater opportunity for being a cheerleader or putting on a game face than in a reorganization situation. Here is a true case study with specific recommendations which you might find helpful.

SITUATION

As part of the governor's effort to streamline government to better serve the citizens of Ohio, the Department of Commerce's Division of Financial Institutions was created. The division reorganized the Division of Banks, Credit Unions and Savings and Loans/Savings Banks into a single coordinated entity. The consolidation forced the reorganization of the management structure as well as the regions.

The major goal was to reduce the annual expenditure of the three former divisions by a significant amount. This would be accomplished in part by reducing the administrative redundancy that resulted from the operation of three relatively small divisions engaged in very similar work. An additional goal of the reorganization was to cross-train examiners to be able to assist other examiners for institutions outside of their areas of specialty.

The division staff's initial response was one of fear for their job security. People were concerned about how the new organizational structure would be implemented. The new superintendent asked for input and received none. The staff wanted to provide input but were unsure of whom to tell. In general, there was a lack of trust and communication between administration and staff.

> Few will have the greatness to bend history itself, but each of us can work to change a small portion of events . . . It is from numberless acts of courage and belief that human history is shaped.
>
> Robert F. Kennedy

As part of the reorganization, all three former divisions met together for their first annual combined conference. I was invited to be speaker for the opening day of the conference. It was my job to help the employees realize the opportunity they had to share information and influence the change process.

Management Strategies: If you are a manager in a similar reorganization situation, here are some strategies for you to consider:

1) Provide avenues for input to the management structure with the caveat being that the director will have the final say. Ask for feedback from those employees who will be directly affected.

2) Develop a newsletter to address the concerns as they arise. Consider including a "Rumor of the Month" section and provide facts to refute the rumor(s).

3) Try to minimize extra layers of management with the new structure.

4) Once the management structure has been defined, allow for focus-group feedback on how to implement the new structure. Allow employees to state their concerns, and try to address those concerns.

5) Provide a flow chart outlining the new responsibilities in the main office so people know whom to contact.

Employee Strategies: If you are an employee in a similar merger situation, here are some strategies for you to consider.

1) Provide constructive feedback on the proposed structure. Give feedback when asked. Volunteer to work on a transition team.

2) Concentrate on doing your job to the best of your ability. Don't waste time on rumors.

3) Ask questions.

4) Develop your own career plan to continue your own growth. Look at all new career options in the new structure. Upgrade skills as needed.

5) Volunteer to be cross-trained.

It's been almost a year since Bryan was diagnosed with Attention Deficit Disorder. I recognize now that last year when Bryan was diagnosed we primarily worked from a boo bird stance. We focused on what Bryan was doing wrong. We were all miserable and discouraged. At the beginning of this school year, I took the *cheerleader* approach. Bryan and I sat down to develop a list of mutual expectations for fourth grade. We designed a plan built on points and rewards given when Bryan meets the expectations. The results have been gratifying. Bryan's grades have improved dramatically. Most importantly — his and our attitudes are much more positive!

We must commit to cheering where we can make a difference. We must put on our game face and get in and play the game even if we feel like we are losing. Robert F. Kennedy summed it up well when he said, "Few will have the greatness to bend history itself, but each of us can work to change a small portion of events . . . It is from numberless acts of courage and belief that human history is shaped." Let's change a small portion of our world and help shape our destiny.

Personal Application Ideas:

 Try some of these tasks as a cheerleader: Give input when none is asked for. Encourage your co-workers when they are discouraged. Volunteer to serve on transition task forces.

 Consider putting on your game face and doing the following:
- keep your attitude positive
- Improve department morale by encouraging cooperation and passing on information
- be kind to others
- show up for work on time
- provide positive feedback to others
- increase your personal productivity and work habits
- control what you say to yourself
- implement skills you've learned (mirroring, whining with purpose, etc.)
- work more efficiently
- increase your quality of work
- ensure your personal safety
- improve your communication (up, down, to co-workers)

ALL STRESSED-OUT AND NO PLACE TO GO

"Initially, I was pleased to have the scope of our services expanded because it adds interest to the job and satisfaction of providing needed assistance. The additional pressure has unfortunately created an environment in which it is impossible to respond promptly to people or interact with them on other than a superficial level. My job is less rewarding to me and I feel less pride in what I am able to accomplish. I am concerned that I have burned out in my job and that it will be difficult for me to maintain a high level of performance."

Social Worker

Do the frustrations in your life stress you? Have the changes in your organization made you feel like you don't fit in anymore? That maybe you never will fit in? I first felt like I didn't fit in when I was in the tenth grade. I was 5' 10" then and still growing. You may recall that the boys in your tenth grade class were not 5' 10". As a result, dating was rare.

I also didn't have a best friend. Aren't ALL high school girls suppose to have a best friend? So, I did what most kids do. I found something to excel in so I would fit in. Well, what do you think a lot of tall girls do to excel in high school? Sports. I was a very good athlete, lettered in three sports, and set several school records in basketball and track.

When I went to college, I took up football . . . tackle football . . . in the snow. In Michigan, the winters were perfect for co-ed tackle football in the snow. Snow football was an exhilarating release of physical energy, a break from studies, and a great place to meet other co-eds. At one of our games, a new guy came to play. Jim. As I lined up against him for the first play, I sized him up (we tall girls learn these skills early on). He was good-looking but too short, I mused to myself. So I tackled him as hard as I could. Once an athlete, you always are competitive.

That was our first physical contact. Time went on. Jim overcame his height disadvantage, and we eventually married. Six years into our marriage, our first son, Bryan, was born. A year later, Jim and I went to a weekend marriage retreat. We both thought we had a great marriage, but we were always interested in ways to improve.

Just prior to this retreat, I read a book called *The Language of Love*. I'm a slow learner because I was just realizing, after seven years of marriage, how men and women sometimes seem to communicate on completely different planes. Have you ever had that experience? This book described a technique for using word pictures or analogies. Word pictures can help people communicate more completely with each other. I thought the marriage retreat would be the perfect opportunity to try my new skill at word pictures.

During one of the exercises, we were each asked to write a description of how we saw our marriage. As I pondered my answer, I thought, "what would be a perfect analogy for our marriage?" It struck me immediately that I should come up with a sports analogy. Jim loves sports and would understand my feelings as a result. I thought to myself, "What is the perfect sport that describes our marriage? Basketball? No. Golf? No. Race car driving — that's it! Our marriage is a lot like a race car team!"

Of course, I'm the race car driver ... I race around as a professional speaker giving speeches and seminars and getting applause. I'm the crowd pleaser. Then, I zoom into the pit (our home), get refueled, rest, and zoom out to my next audience. Jim is my pit crew. He's there to be my support, to take care of our sons and the nitty gritty details of running the business while also working a full-time job for the insurance benefits. It was perfect. From my experience, it described our marriage at that point. I proudly wrote out a very colorful description and exchanged my notebook with Jim. I watched out of the corner of my eye to see if he liked my word picture. I waited to see his reaction . . . no reaction. That should have been my first clue that something was wrong!

He slowly put my book down, took a deep breath, and sighed. Then he said, "This is it? That's all I am to you ... the pit crew?!?" And at that moment, it hit me. It was true. All the discussions we had came flooding back to me. We argued at how stressed our lives had become due to my lack of prioritizing. Jim felt like I treated him as my last priority. In fact, I had been treating Jim like my pit crew. During our discussions, I had always defended myself. I rationalized that it was stressful running a business, and yes, of course, he was a priority. But my actions certainly spoke a lot louder than my words.

And there, at that marriage retreat, I realized that I needed Jim to know that. I needed to know right then and there if Jim could love me in spite of my self-centered nature. All my life, I performed for other people so I would fit in. Sports and music all gained me love and acceptance from my family and peers. I never had experienced true unconditional love just for whom I was, and I needed to know if Jim would choose to love me in spite of me.

I also knew at that moment that if Jim chose to love me, I wanted to give myself permission to be the kind of woman I wanted to be and the kind of wife Jim deserved. That day I found out that Jim chose to love me . . . even though the truth about me had come out. Jim might have been my pit crew, but until I told the truth, I was the one who was "in the pits" and stressed-out from trying to please everyone.

> *"Change generally equates to more duties not less and therefore trying to accomplish all the necessary task sometimes exposes the ugly head of stress."*
>
> *Quality Improvement Manager*

Recognizing the truth about myself was difficult because it required that I change my behavior. For most people, change is incredibly stressful, whether at home or work. Whether you start a new business as I had or whether your company is being merged — both require major adjustments in our life. Our priorities can get confused. Our work quality and performance can suffer. It takes a physical toll on us — leaving us all stressed-out with no place to go.

More than 200 million workdays are lost each year nationwide due to employee stress, anxiety, and depression. According to the National Mental Health Association, the fallout from stress and depression (absenteeism, employee turnover, and lower productivity) accounts for about $200 to $300 billion in lost revenue for American companies every year.

> ✆ *"The staff generally seemed to agree that the reorganization coupled with "all the changes going on throughout the agency" has created an "enormous" level of stress in the department. As . one person put it, "You could make a comparison to taking a hammer out and hitting yourself in the head with it. The first few times it's going to hurt like heck, but after a while you're just going to get numb to the pain." I just wonder if maybe people are just kind of getting used to being stressed. You eventually don't even realize the stress you have on you anymore . . . it leads to a state of frustration. It might be just something that builds and builds and builds, and then one day you think to yourself, "I don't want to work here anymore."*
>
> *Project Leader*

The National Study of the Changing Workforce found that 88 percent of the employees surveyed reported having to work hard and 68 percent having to work fast, yet 60 percent still don't have enough time to get it all done. So, that means more than half the people feel they don't have enough time to get their jobs done. A very high percentage — 71 percent — said they feel used up at the end of the day, and 57 percent reported being burned out or stressed by work.

There are two types of stress we can experience. Short-term or acute stress is usually caused by one major change event or stressor. Acute stress is a reaction to an immediate threat or current event. It's called "short-term stress" because it typically takes you a relatively short period of time to recover. Unfortunately, many of us are dealing with chronic stress, or ongoing stress. Our reality is that we are struggling to deal with multiple change events simultaneously. Work changes coupled with changes in our personal lives can cause pressure that may seem unrelenting. The result is a much more extended period of time needed for recovery. Too much stress can appear in the form of illness or fatigue. Remember, seventy-one percent of people surveyed say they feel "used up" at the end of the day.

> *"I am negatively stressed because of the changes. I'm exhausted from trying to conform to work environment changes. I feel less productive and less motivated. As a result, I'm more prone to using my sick leave time."*
>
> *Director of EEO*

Many times the change itself is not a "bad" change, but the increased workload often increases our stress level. Sometimes we are pleased to have the scope of our jobs expanded because it adds interest to the job and increased job satisfaction. However, the additional pressure that comes with increased job scope unfortunately can create an environment in which it is impossible to respond promptly to our customers. Therefore, our job ends up being less rewarding to us. Our pride is affected in terms of what we are able to accomplish. The result can be burnout, which makes it increasingly difficult for us to maintain a high level of job performance.

RATE YOUR STRESS SYMPTOMS

Check any of the following stress symptoms that you've experienced in the last 8–12 months:

Physical Symptoms:

__ headaches	__ fatigue
__ appetite change	__ weight change
__ insomnia	__ constipation
__ tight/dry throat	__ diarrhea
__ lower back pain	__ hives/skin rash
__ indigestion	__ menstrual distress
__ aching neck and shoulders	__ shortness of breath
__ heartburn	__ shaky hands
__ increased heart rate	__ chest pain
__ high blood pressure	__ muscle tension
__ grinding teeth	

Emotional Symptoms:

__ anxiety   __ nervousness
__ irritability   __ anger
__ apathy   __ withdrawal/apathy
__ sense of inadequacy   __ reduced motivation
__ emotionally drained   __ nightmares
__ excessive daydreaming   __ diminished memory/recall
__ loss of sense of humor   __ mood swings
__ excessive spending   __ low self-esteem
__ excessive sleeping   __ poor concentration
__ overeating   __ defensiveness

Behavioral Symptoms:

__ absenteeism
__ shirking responsibilities
__ reduced productivity
__ reduced quality of performance
__ inappropriate hostility or outbursts of temper
__ inappropriate mistrust of others
__ increased smoking
__ missing appointments or deadlines
__ minor accidents/increased errors
__ indecisiveness
__ working later and more obsessively than usual
__ sexual or romantic indiscretions
__ change in close family relationships
__ problems with sexual performance
__ use of mood-altering drugs
__ excessive use of alcohol or tobacco
__ inability to concentrate
__ impatience
__ procrastination
__ poor personal hygiene

The more of these symptoms you checked, the more potential you have for chronic stress. If you have concerns about the number of symptoms you are experiencing, you may want to check with a health care professional. Only a professional would be able to diagnose what these symptoms may mean for you.

GAME FACE CONDITIONING PLAN

Remember that putting on a "Game Face" means taking action on the things you can control. You can control how you deal with stress. You may ask, "Why bother? A little stress doesn't hurt anyone." We already have looked at the incredible monetary risks to an organization due to absenteeism. More shocking than that is the fact that research on the relationship between health and emotion indicates that stress affects the body at the cellular level in ways that increase the risk of disease. Stress is linked to heart disease and hypertension, and may even play a role in cancer.

We must commit ourselves to a plan of action that will help fight off the ugly symptoms of stress. You may want to include some or all of the following components in your plan: fitness, forty winks, focus, food, fellowship, and fun.

"The changes have created a lot of opportunities for people who want to change. It is hard even when you think the changes are for the best. It is hard when you are unsure if the changes will last for very long. It is exciting, invigorating, and draining all at the same time."

Director of Data Service

FITNESS

Regular exercise can really make a difference as a stress reducer. Neuroscience researchers at Rockefeller University found that regular, moderate exercise is probably the best way to counteract the effects of stress. Physical activity can reduce the insulin levels that are naturally raised by stress, and exercise also lowers blood pressure and the heart's resting rate.

Most experts suggest a minimum of 20 minutes of cardiovascular exercise three times per week. Consider how many of us own a piece of exercise equipment and have good intentions but don't follow through and use it. Let's dust off that exercise equipment and start doing something that will have positive short- and long-term effects on our health and well-being.

Aside from the physical well-being benefits, people also report that exercise can help you think more creatively. Exercise gives you more energy. The problem is that we never get beyond the pain of exercise to the point where we reap the energy benefits. The benefits of exercise do not happen overnight.

For many years I didn't exercise because I didn't have a weight problem or any specific health concerns. I still don't have a weight problem, but now I exercise simply because it's right for me. I feel better and have more energy. It feels good to know I'm doing something now that will reap many benefits as I age.

Exercise is a lot like saving money — it's painful initially (we'd rather spend than save), and it doesn't seem as if it makes much of a difference. Yet, we all know that with compound interest, a little money saved now can reap huge dividends down the road. Exercise for the stress reliever that it is, and know that it is an investment in your future health.

FORTY WINKS

Regular Sleep Routine

We need seven nights of good restful sleep per week. Some people need more sleep than others, but most sleep experts believe that adults need eight hours of sleep per night. Ongoing research is showing that when people don't get enough sleep, they build up "sleep debt." The debt accumulates night after night. If you get one hour of sleep less per night, after eight nights you have built up a sleep debt equivalent to one night's sleep. Sleep debt takes a toll on our motor and intellectual functions. William Dement, author of *The Promise of Sleep*, says, "In the simplest of terms, a large sleep debt makes you stupid." It takes a toll on us in terms of work errors and can make us emotionally distant from our co-workers, friends, and family.

> *We define an adequate quantity of sleep as that amount which, when you attain it on a steady basis, produces a full degree of daytime alertness and feeling of well-being the following day.*
>
> John W. Shepard, M.D.
> Mayo Clinic Sleep
> Disorders Clinic

The University of Chicago studied young men who slept only four hours per night for six nights and found that sleep deprivation adversely affected their metabolism and hormone functions. The effects resembled those normally found in the aging process. Researchers believe that the effects of sleep deprivation might possibly increase the severity of chronic disorders as people age.

Another interesting point about sleep is that our body needs a regular sleep-wake routine. For those of us with daytime working hours, most of us go to bed at a certain time and get up at a certain time. On the weekends, however, we tend to go to bed later and sleep in. Here's the problem — if we sleep an extra hour beyond our normal waking time, we will be tired. It then takes our body forty-eight hours to recover from sleeping late. Let's say you normally wake up at 6:30 a.m.. However, on Saturday, you get up after 7:45 a.m. Because you slept in that extra hour plus, it will take your body literally two days or 48 hours to recover. You will feel tired. We often refer to Mondays as "Blue Monday." Perhaps that is in part due to the fact that we are still recovering from "sleeping in."

Sleep experts suggest you should get up within an hour of your normal waking period even if you go to bed later than usual. To make up for those later nights, consider taking a twenty-minute nap in the afternoon. To make up your sleep debt, it is best to go to bed earlier than to sleep later. Aside from the physical benefits from your sleep routine, imagine how much you can enjoy the quiet time in your house with no one awake. Forty winks can make a big difference.

The Mayo Clinic Health Letter suggests the following habits so you can increase the amount of sleep you get each night:

- Use a VCR to tape your favorite late shows so you can watch them earlier the next day.

- Use a personalized browser to scan the Internet for you rather than surfing all night.

- Find the local weather information, sports scores, or other timely items on the World Wide Web instead of staying up for the late TV news.

- Watch less television.

WAKING UP

Think about how you wake up in the morning. Many of us wake up to an alarm clock. By virtue of the name, what does "alarm" say

Many of us wake up to an alarm clock. By virtue of the name, what does "alarm" say to us? Danger! We rise in the morning to a danger signal.

to us? Danger! We rise in the morning to a danger signal. We get out of bed, running around like a mad person. We yank the kids out of bed, shove a pastry at them. Oops! We forgot their lunch so we throw them some money. While they are running out of the house, we yell, "Have a good day!" We rush to work. When we arrive, we think, "Okay, I made it!" But in what condition? Some of us are stressed-out before we even get to work.

Experts believe that the first 15 minutes of your waking time set the tone for the rest of the day. During the first 15 minutes you are awake, your subconscious mind is at work because you are not totally conscious at this point. Some of us are completely stressed out in the first 15 minutes we are awake. Consider the difference it would make if you would wake up 15 minutes earlier and wake up to music or a natural-light lamp instead of an alarm clock. A natural light lamp slowly fills your bedroom with light just like natural light so you wake up naturally.

What are you listening to or watching when you get up? Do you watch the news? Why do we listen to the news? It's rarely positive and won't help you focus on the good things in life. Why do we listen to the traffic report when we're already stuck in traffic? It's too late. If we're going to get into a major traffic snarl, it's not like we're going to get to work on time by listening to the news at that point. Why not listen to beautiful and uplifting music or your favorite speaker or comedian?

> ✺ *"I would like it if the leadership of the organization would understand that many people are in new positions and still learning. The pace that has always been kept before cannot continue simply because the new people have not fully adjusted to their jobs. Not only is the same work pace expected to be continued, but a whole new realm of additional work is being added because of the new leadership and ideas. This causes tremendous personal stress and organizational chaos."*
>
> *Department Chair*

FOCUS

Meditation

Herbert Benson has demonstrated in his research that while chronic stress is harmful to the body, daily meditation can reduce stress and promote relaxation and overall well-being. Even Carl Jung went so far as to say that spirituality was such an essential ingredient in psychological health that he could heal only those middle-aged people who embraced a spiritual or religious perspective toward life.

> Dr. Herbert Benson found that praying affects epinephrine and other corticosteroid messengers or stress hormones, leading to lower blood pressure, more relaxed heart rate and respiration and other benefits.
>
> Claudia Wallis
> Time magazine

Meditation is a way of quieting your mind and increasing your ability to focus and concentrate. This is done by blocking out distractions and focusing your attention on one thing at a time. This process not only calms your mind but calms your body as well. The result is a more tranquil mental and physical state of well-being. Meditation can counteract the effects of stress on your body.

Meditation elicits a specific set of physiologic changes: decreased metabolism and heart rate, easier breathing, and distinctively slower brain waves. Recent research demonstrates that stress hormones have a direct impact on the body's immunological defenses against disease. "Anything involved with meditation and controlling the state of mind that alters hormone activity has the potential to have an impact on the immune systems," states David Felton, chairman of the Department of Neurobiology at the University of Rochester.

Consider meditating during the first fifteen minutes you are awake to set the tone for your day. My typical morning routine includes reading my Bible, praying, exercising, and then showering and readying myself for the day. I have found that my faith in God has been my only rock and fortress throughout all the changes that have occurred in my life. When all feels unstable around me, I have confidence that God is the same yesterday, today, and tomorrow. On what is your confidence built?

Perhaps your meditation time will include yoga or deep-breathing techniques. Maybe a good start for your day is to read an inspirational book in the morning or to write in your journal. Choose a routine that fits your beliefs and comfort level and begin reaping the mental, emotional, and physical benefits of meditation.

FOOD

Watch what you put into your mouth. There are some things that we eat which can increase our stress levels. I'm not a dietician, so I won't be recommending any specific diets, but there are five foods I would suggest you avoid.

FIGHT OR FLIGHT FOODS

The consumption of foods containing chemicals that trigger fright or flight will increase your stress. Here are some of the offenders: coffee, tea, cola, chocolate, and many non-cola drinks. Even some types of nuts contain caffeine. We have total control over what we put in our mouths. We need to ask ourselves, will what I'm drinking or eating increase my heart rate, increase my blood pressure, cause anxiety, irritability, or stomach acid?

You may be thinking, "You don't want to see me without my caf-

> Water is second only to pure oxygen for dissipating stress.

feine in the morning!" What we don't realize is that caffeine is merely borrowing energy from our future. Once we fuel ourselves with a proper diet, we won't require the artificial effects of caffeine to get us through our day. Eliminating caffeine for some of you would be a major struggle. Don't feel that you need to eliminate caffeine all at once. Know that you may have to endure suffering from withdrawal headaches for one to two weeks until the caffeine is out of your system. However, the long-term benefits far outweigh the short-term pain. Many people report increased energy, better sleep at night, and decreased irritability and jitteryness after eliminating caffeine from their diet.

There are many alternatives to caffeine. The best alternative is water. Lots of water.

Do you realize that the first sign of dehydration is a headache? Stress triggers dehydration in the body, which in turn amplifies into feelings of fatigue. Water is second only to pure oxygen for dissipating stress. Do you suffer from headaches? Perhaps it is because you're not drinking enough water. We should start our day with an eight-ounce glass of water. Here's a simple remedy: when you're taking a shower in the morning, drink in some of that warm water. Sure, some of you are thinking, "how disgusting!" Realize that ice-cold water constricts your blood vessels. Warm water is much better for you. You'll be so much better off if the first liquid you pick up is water rather than caffeine.

DEPLETION OF VITAMIN B

B-complex vitamins are critically important to our body in times of stress. When we are under stress, our body naturally depletes the B vitamins from our system. Additionally, there are some foods that contribute to the depletion of B vitamins: those containing refined white sugar and processed flour. When we lack B vitamins in our body, the effects include anxiety and depression. Personally, I know I'm stressed when I get depressed. When I get depressed, I want to sleep a lot, which means I'm not very productive. It can be an ugly cycle.

Consider eating meat, whole grain, green leafy vegetables, and legumes. All contain B-complex vitamins which are important in stressful times. You may also consider taking vitamin B supplements if you know you are not eating in a way that will replenish the vitamins you are losing.

Hypoglycemia or Low Blood Sugar

When you eat in a way that causes hypoglycemia, or low blood sugar, your blood sugar skyrockets and then crashes. The drop in your blood-sugar level can cause anxiety, headaches, dizziness, nausea, and trembling. The biggest offenders include consuming high amounts of sugar over a short period of time and skipping meals.

Jack Groppel, a sports scientist, fitness expert, and author of *The Anti-Diet Book,* finds that a good night's sleep depletes much of the glycogen stored in the liver (glycogen is the starch the body converts to glucose for energy). The brain works on two things: oxygen and glucose. If your glycogen storage is empty by morning, you must eat something for breakfast in order for you to function at a high level. Several studies show that eating breakfast is associated with improved midmorning endurance and with better attitudes toward work.

> Eating breakfast is associated with improved midmorning endurance and with better attitudes toward work.
> Jack Groppel
> *The Anti-Diet Book*

How can you think, be creative, or solve problems when you haven't put any fuel into your system? Breakfast is the number one meal that we should be eating. Dinner is the largest meal we tend to eat, but it's the meal we can most afford to skip. You are what you eat — what does your diet say about you?

Often in the late afternoon hours, we feel low energy. We naturally go for some sugar to give us more energy. What we don't realize is that the immediate lift we experience is usually followed by fatigue. It's better to steer clear of sweets and instead commit yourself to eating well-balanced, low-sugar meals on a reasonable schedule. For quick and steady energy throughout the day, eat lots of fresh fruits.

Salt

Salt is critical to your body's functioning, yet too much salt can raise your blood pressure. Use a salt substitute, or even better go without. Pay attention to the sodium content on packages, and limit your salt intake.

ASPARTAME

One of the biggest controversies surrounding nutrition is the debate about the safety and effects of aspartame, more commonly known as NutraSweet. There are many websites and articles written on both sides of the argument. I included it because of the experience of several friends as a warning for you to go and research for yourself whether aspartame may be contributing to the stress symptoms in your life.

When we consume any unnatural chemicals in our foods, such as aspartame or NutraSweet, we don't know the effect it will have on us. There are ninety-two documented results of what happens when people have consumed aspartame, including numbness, headaches, dizziness, fatigue, irritability, nausea, weight gain, depression, memory loss, and joint pain. I have two different friends who drank two to four diet sodas a day containing aspartame. Both suffered for many years from fibromyalgia, a condition affecting seven to ten million Americans. The fibromyalgia symptoms include widespread muscular pain and fatigue. When my friends stopped drinking the diet drinks, within two weeks their symptoms disappeared.

Be aware that aspartame can be found in almost all diet drinks and food; in some children's cereals, vitamins, and sweet drinks; and even in some kinds of yogurt. Please do the research for yourself on aspartame, or simply abstain from ingesting aspartame for a period of time and see if you notice a difference for yourself physically.

"I just changed jobs. This is always a very stressful transition. I would like a way to deal with change so that I could adjust and relax a little more. The job change has put a lot of pressure on me. It makes me sad, angry and happy at the same time. I can't wait until I feel comfortable and confident of myself again."

Office Support Specialist

FELLOWSHIP

The Journal of the American Medical Association in 1997 reported that a lack of diverse social contacts was a stronger risk factor for colds than smoking, low vitamin C intake, or elevated stress hormones. The Carnegie Mellon University researchers who conducted the study say that interacting with a wide range of people likely tempers our physical response to stressful situations. They suspect that social support may somehow boost immune function.

Social isolation — having no one to confide in — is a serious source of stress for many. We have become so busy, we haven't made the time to develop friendships with others. That is why some find it incredibly stressful to consider retirement. We haven't developed any friendships or hobbies that will give us something to do with our extra time. We need to begin preparing for retirement far before we actually retire. We are created as human beings, not human doings, human havings, or human goings. Yet, much of our worldly success is defined by what we "do" or "have." In the end, we will all die and leave all we have on this earth. What are you doing today to invest in the important relationships in your life? Although I have written several books and spoken to thousands of people across the country, I know that the greatest measure of my success will be how Jim and I have raised our two sons, not the "things" I have accomplished. This is difficult to keep in mind while on the treadmill of success.

We need to take time out of our busy, stress-filled lives to connect with family and friends. Having someone to confide in is important both on and off our jobs. Often, our friends and family members can help us resolve problems and help relieve our stress.

To face the frustrations of working in a changing organization, we must develop the light approach to life.

> When our lives are defined only in terms of the fruits of action, the circumstances of our lives define us. In this state of identity, we are fragile, vulnerable, and at-risk...We have become human doers who have lost connection to our heritage as human beings.
>
> Kevin Cashman
> Executive Coach

FUN

To face the frustrations of dealing with constant change, we must devel-

We are created as human beings — not human doings, human havings, or human goings.

op the light approach to life. This is an area I constantly have to work on. One of the things I learned at that marriage retreat is how important having fun is to Jim. I married him in part because of his sense of humor and ability to "smell the roses" along life's journey. Although I use a lot of humor in my speaking, I'm a fairly intense workaholic. I love what I do — work is fun for me. Therefore, I don't have a lot of need for fun. As a result, taking time out of my schedule to have fun with Jim or our boys is a commitment I have to make. Since I'm a natural-born scheduler, I schedule monthly "date nights" with Jim. When it works well, Jim and the boys travel with me to a speaking engagement. I love to speak and Jim and the boys have fun in whatever location we are — I join them for fun evening activities, or we spend an extra day sight-seeing. It's a win/win.

What are you doing to incorporate more "fun" into your life?

Ken Blanchard, author of *The One Minute Manager*, uses a perspective-setting technique he calls the "zoo mentality." He developed it when his children were growing up. Blanchard noticed that whenever he was at a park or zoo, there would be parents yelling at their kids for running around, misbehaving, and generally having a great time. It seemed ironic to him to take children to a place to have fun and then yell at them. So, Blanchard decided he would get into a "zoo men-

> "Nourishing the soul" means making sure I attend to those things that give my life rich-ness and depth of meaning.
> Robert Fulghum

tality." If his kids started acting silly or chasing each other, he would join in the fun. Now he uses that skill at his company's management meetings.

How is your sense of humor? Gauge your sense of humor by answering true or false to each of the following statements.

Sense of Humor Inventory:

1. __ I frequently laugh during the day.
2. __ I read the comic section of the local newspaper each day.
3. __ I look for cartoons and quips in my reading.
4. __ I repeat to my friends and associates stories that make me laugh.
5. __ I seek out funny movies.
6. __ I feel comfortable sharing embarrassing moments with friends and co-workers.
7. __ I am able to laugh at my silly mistakes.
8. __ I collect examples of humor in cartoons, tapes, jokes, etc.
9. __ I enjoy playing with children.
10. __ I consider myself a person who enjoys levity.

If you answered *false* more than three times, your sense of humor needs works. People who take themselves too seriously often have a difficult time establishing easy, enjoyable relationships with others. If you have a hard time letting loose, try to gradually make some changes. The next time you make an embarrassing mistake, laugh it off. Or practice telling a funny story that you enjoyed hearing. You'll find that lightheartedness can be contagious — both to others and yourself.

Improving Your Sense of Humor

A sense of humor is learned, not an innate, trait. Here are some ways to get your laugh mechanism in working order.

- *Redefine how you react to things.* Try to find the light aspects even in serious situations. Ponder what was embarrassing for you years ago and reframe your view of it to see the funny side.

- *Consider that being childlike can sometimes be beneficial.* Seek to recapture some of the joy and wonderment you experienced as a child. When our son Drew was three and a half years old, he was running errands with his dad. While they were driving along, Drew noticed a squirrel lying in the road and asked his dad, "Is that a squirrel?" To which Jim replied, "Yes, it is." Drew somberly asked, "Is he dead?" "Yes, he's dead, Drew." Drew thought about that for a moment and quietly said, "He must not have looked both ways."

> To face the frustrations of working in a changing organization, we must develop the light approach to life.

- *Take humor breaks.* We take lunch breaks, coffee breaks, and exercise breaks; we can accent the light side of life by taking humor breaks. A humor break could be reading the newspaper's comic section, getting together with a friend who makes you laugh, or watching one of your favorite comedies.

  We keep a log of funny things our boys say as they are growing up. The boys love reading those funny stories and lines. It re-creates the humorous moments we treasure as a family. Program yourself to laugh at regular times just as you program yourself to sleep a certain number of hours.

- *Give more than you take.* People-oriented individuals tend to think more of others than themselves and thus do not take themselves too seriously. Strive to be people-oriented. Make yourself do a kind deed for someone each day.

- *Share your humor.* When people hear you tell a funny story or repeat a caption of a cartoon, they will look at you differently and will be more likely to have fun with you. Remembering a funny anecdote to tell someone will help you keep in mind the humorous side of life. Keep in mind that poking fun at yourself is where true humor comes from — not making fun of someone's race or gender. Most people enjoy funny true stories more than a joke.

- *Build a laugh library.* Assemble a collection of your favorite humor writers, cartoons, records, tapes, and jokes. Two of my favorite "funny people" are Bill Cosby and Liz Curtis Higgs. Both relate hysterically funny true stories that happened to them. Liz is a fellow professional speaker and author who has just released her first historical comedy novel, *Mixed Signals* — a don't-miss read!

> *The ability to laugh at life is right at the top, with love and communication, in the hierarchy of our needs. Humor has much to do with pain; it exaggerates the anxieties and absurdities we feel, so that we gain distance and through laughter, relief.*
> Sara Davidson

- *Be playful.* Look for humor behind words, associations, and situations.

SLOW DOWN AND SMELL THE ROSES

University of Maryland sociologist John Robinson has noticed a progressive increase in our hurriedness over the years. In 1965, 25% of those surveyed said their lives were rushed all the time. By 1985, the figure had climbed to 32%. More recently, in 1992, the number had risen to 38%. That is almost a fifty percent increase from 1965. Interestingly, those people who lived in small towns felt as rushed as those who lived in big cities. For both groups, they felt their lives were hurried not only at work but also at play.

If we are going to lessen the hurriedness of our rapidly changing lives, we need to define the kind of life we want — personally and professionally. Stephen Bertman, author of *Hyperculture: The Human Cost of Speed*, suggests that we restrain our technology by turning off the television and computer. We must keep connected to our history by keeping our family memories alive, celebrating ethnic traditions and religious rituals. Finally, Bertman suggests we regain our senses by taking walks and enjoying nature. He believes that we must come to see that "slow" in not necessarily bad, nor is "fast" necessarily good.

I think Bertman would appreciate this poem someone sent me via the Internet. The author is unknown. It's a good reminder for each of us in our stressful, high-change lifestyles to pay attention to the important things in life.

> *Mirth is like a flash of lightning that breaks through a gloom of clouds, and glitters for a moment: cheerfulness keeps up a kind of day-light in the mind, and fills it with a steady and perpetual serenity.*
>
> Joseph Addison

Slow Dance

Have you ever watched kids on a merry-go-round
Or listened to the rain slapping on the ground?

Ever followed a butterfly's erratic flight
Or gazed at the sun into the fading night?

You better slow down, don't dance so fast
Time is short. The music won't last

Do you run through each day on the fly
When you ask, "How are you?" Do you hear the reply?

When the day is done, do you lie in your bed
With the next hundred chores running through your head?

You'd better slow down, don't dance so fast
Time is short, the music won't last

Ever told your child, We'll do it tomorrow
And in your haste not see his sorrow?

Ever lost touch, Let a good friendship die
'cause you never had time to call and say "Hi"?

You'd better slow down, don't dance so fast
Time is short. The music won't last

When you run so fast to get somewhere
You miss the fun of getting there

When you worry and hurry through your day
It is like an unopened gift . . . thrown away.

Life is not a race. Do take it slower
Hear the music before the song is over

Personal Application Ideas:

 Develop and stick to a regular fitness routine.

 Determine how much sleep you require. Take control of your sleep: use a VCR to tape your favorite late shows so you can watch them earlier the next day; use a personalized browser to scan the Internet for you rather than surfing all night; find the local weather information, sports scores, or other timely items on the World Wide Web instead of staying up for the late TV news.

 Get up fifteen minutes earlier than usual so you can have time for meditation and to eat a quick breakfast.

 Decide what foods you need to eliminate and add to your diet in order to lessen your stress response.

 Name three good friends who are outside your family. Make a "date" now to spend time with them during the next month. Write a personal note or e-mail a friend you haven't spoken to in awhile. Don't forget to "date" your significant other so they remain "significant."

 Develop your sense of humor by: (a) redefining how you react to things; (b) seeking to recapture some of the joy and wonderment you experienced as a child; (c) taking humor breaks; (d) striving to be people-oriented; (e) make yourself do a kind deed for someone else each day; (f) sharing your humor with others; (g) building a laugh library; or (h) looking for humor behind words, associations, and situations.

WHEN THE GOING GETS TOUGH, THE TOUGH GET TALKING

"I would like to be able to be enthusiastic every day about my job and my responsibilities as a committee chair and feel that I do make an impact on our working environment and being able to juggle both roles. Some days I feel like "what the heck — no one really cares any way! I'd like to replace fear with something more positive."

Secretary

I was both excited and nervous! I had just been offered a contract with a national public seminar company, and I was 27 years old. Could I really do this? Throughout my professional career I had taken jobs that were slightly above my skill level — would this be the time I wouldn't be successful? This was my dream: to become a professional speaker. It was the goal I had been working toward.

I had four months to prepare myself for my first public seminar to be delivered in Chicago. It was critical that I change what I was saying to myself to overcome my fear of failure. So, I wrote down the following statement, "I am a national professional speaker." I repeated this statement on the drive to my current job as a corporate trainer and on the drive home. I must have repeated this positive self-talk statement thousands of time. On the days I didn't feel real-

> You must be the change you want to see in the world.
> Mahatma Gandhi

ly positive, I could almost imagine someone looking over my shoulder saying, "Who, you? You're way too young and inexperienced!"

After four months of convincing myself I was a national professional speaker, I walked into that hotel meeting room in Chicago and had the confidence to do a great job. I delivered the program like the professional speaker I had envisioned. I felt great when the day was over!

Later, I asked the training director of the public seminar company whether or not he ever questioned my ability to speak because of my age. He said to me, "Patti, because it was never a question in your mind, I knew it would never be a question in your seminar participants' minds." Aha! What a breakthrough that moment was for me.

In Chapter 9 we discussed the fact that "you are what you eat." I believe it's just as important that "you are what you think." In computer circles they talk about "garbage in, garbage out." This is equally true in our lives. So, what are you saying to yourself about your organizational change? What are you saying about YOU and how you feel about the change(s)?

What we say to ourselves — our self-talk — in large part determines how we will feel about the changes taking place. One of my favorite quotations of Eleanor Roosevelt is, "No one can make you feel inferior without your consent." In change situations, no one can make you resistant without your consent. No one can make you bitter without your consent. No one can make you angry without your consent. The bottom line is that we OWN our own thoughts and feelings. What we think and how we feel is totally up to us.

> No one can make you feel inferior without your consent.
> Eleanor Roosevelt

Perhaps some of us talk to ourselves because we have some kind of audience in mind. Even if nobody hears us or responds to our concerns, it's somehow reassuring to know that our woes have been heard. Sometimes we're our own most sympathetic listener.

Dan Teitelbaum, author of the book *Mental Toughness in Corporate America,* found that psychological studies have shown that low performers tend to focus on the past and the defeats they've sustained, average performers keep their attention only on the here

What we say to ourselves — our self-talk — in large part determines how we will feel about the changes taking place.

and now, and top performers stay focused on the future. These top performers are riveted on the specific future victories they're planning to make happen. Not only are they focused on what they want to achieve, they also keep telling themselves that they can and will make it happen.

Teitelbaum likens our subconscious mind to a computer's hard drive. Our subconscious mind is like a computer's RAM memory with several software applications running beneath the surface.

Throughout the day, we click on various icons which are the tasks we are completing. Our brain is capable of doing several tasks (or having several programs running) simultaneously. Unless, of course we get a computer virus which shuts down our entire system. Negative thinking is much like a computer virus — it affects everything we do, how we act, and our future capabilities. If we are "running" around with negative thoughts, we must find a way to overwrite the old, negative beliefs contained in our brain's hard drive with new, confident, positive self-talk.

CHANGING WHAT WE SAY TO OURSELVES

One powerful way to counteract negative effects of change is to change how we think and what we believe about ourselves and our situation. This changes our internal hard drive's thought processes. These thoughts have a tremendous impact on the outcome of our situation. If we change our thoughts, often we can change how we perceive our situation.

A simple formula to demonstrate this is:

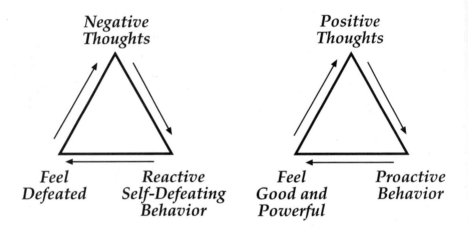

Let's look at an example . . . Two people can encounter the same traffic jam and have two completely opposite outcomes. Becky is a "type A" driver who races to each traffic light and is always speeding. When she encounters a traffic snarl, she blames the traffic jam on all the "incompetent" drivers out there. As a result, she weaves in and out of traffic and takes side roads to try and bypass the jam. The consequence for Becky is that by the time she reaches her job at 8:06 a.m., she is experiencing high blood pressure and fatigue and feels defeated before she begins her workday.

George, in contrast to Becky, always drives at the speed limit and considers himself a safe driver. When he encounters a traffic snarl, he thinks to himself that it is simply a matter of time before the traffic is clear. He chooses to enjoy the extra time provided him with an opportunity to listen to his favorite tapes or radio station. The consequence? George arrives at his job at 8:09 a.m. relaxed and ready to begin the day's work. It all began with their thought life.

NEGATIVE SELF-TALK ATTITUDES

Self-talk is the stream of conscious thought that reflects our attitude toward a stressful situation or person. Self-talk and our beliefs often make for a self-fulfilling prophecy. Therefore, it is vital that we control what we say to ourselves.

Negative self-talk can contribute to our feeling overwhelmed and defeated by those who criticize us. If we allow someone else to determine how we feel about ourselves, we give him or her the power to control our reaction to change. We must realize that change in itself is neither negative nor positive unless we attribute meaning to it. We DO possess complete control over the meaning we attribute to change and, therefore, how we will respond to it.

> I believe that the worst of all spiritual defeats is to lose enthusiasm for life's possibilities.
> Nathaniel Branden

Robert Anthony states it so well when he says, "If you don't change your beliefs, your life will be like this forever. Is that good news?" That's a great question. What would your answer be?

Self-talk begins inside each one of us. We cannot control the effects that change has on us. However, we CAN control what we say to ourselves while in the throes of change. Let me provide you with a list of some of the attitudes that contribute to negative self-talk. Let's see if any of these sound familiar.

ALL-OR-NOTHING THINKING

Things are black and white. If your performance is not perfect, you see yourself as a total failure. Perfectionism can be a serious block to good self-esteem and can be a cause of depression. All-or-nothing thinking can cause emotional stress and prevent us from being happy. In many ways, perfectionistic thinking will set us up to be disappointed because consistently achieving "all" is impossible. Be realistic. Change your expectations.

The organizational change you are in the midst of will, in all likelihood, not have a perfect outcome. It will not achieve all it was designed to achieve. Have realistic expectations, and you will probably experience less anxiety and disappointment, both professionally and personally.

MENTAL FILTER

You pick out a single negative detail and dwell on it exclusively. I recall reading an article about the management guru Rosabeth Moss Kanter, a professor at Harvard University who has written numerous books. The article pointed out that after she has finished giving a speech, she reads the evaluations. She is crushed if several are not positive. She ignores the hundreds of positive comments and focuses on the few negative perceptions. If this happens to someone like Kanter, we can all fall prey to this negative mental filter.

DISQUALIFYING THE POSITIVE

You don't give credit for any positive results to the change initiative. You also tend to attribute positive experiences to something other than your own abilities. In other words, you don't perceive the situation accurately. Here is a typical phrase you might hear from someone who disqualifies the positive: "The increased profits didn't come as a result of the reorganization. The economy improved and all business profits are up." Only an economist could really analyze to what extent the reorganization contributed to the bottom line. Regardless, we need to be open and willing to celebrate any successes that might be attributed to organizational changes.

When being praised for leading a major change initiative, you say, "Oh, it's no big deal. The department really did most of the work with the project. It really is a credit to our entire department." Disqualifying the positive can become a professional trap. People will only continue to give us positive feedback if we accept it. No one wants to try to convince us that we were the effective

> Most folks are about as happy as they make up their minds to be.
> Abraham Lincoln

leader in the change initiative. Since we don't believe we are effective, why should anyone else? Often promotions are given to those ready and willing to accept their abilities and take credit when it is deserved.

JUMPING TO CONCLUSIONS

You anticipate that things will turn out badly, and you are convinced that your prediction is fact. This is particularly true for me with technology changes. When I convince myself that I am never going to be able to learn how to use the new technology, I usually do struggle with my learning curve. With difficult audiences, I have to force myself to visualize only success with them or my nervousness as a speaker is sure to come through. The result is then less than satisfactory.

> If you had a choice, would you enjoy hanging around you? Tune in to your inner talk. Ultimately, the way you talk to yourself determines your attitudes, actions, and degree of success in life.
> Lynn B. Sanders

How about your new "pirate leader"? Have you jumped to the conclusion that she or he doesn't like you and won't be effective? Our boys' elementary school got a new principal this year. We loved our former principal, who was promoted into administration — she knew everyone by name, obviously loved children, and was an effective parent advocate. I knew I wasn't going to like the new principal. She was too perky and "fake." Why did she automatically change the recognition program for the children? I liked last year's system better — if it ain't broke, why fix it? All of us have the tendency to jump to conclusions and fear the unknown when it comes to change.

> "When I think of change, I think of fear. Fear of trying something new. Fear of leaving old friends to move on and up the career chain. I really feel that success doesn't happen in the absence of fear, but rather in spite of it. Risk is scary and it is exhilirating. Taking a risk and meeting change head on allows you to see many other opportunities, to experience life in a new way, to learn, grow, and it allows you to become all you were meant to be."
> *Administrative Specialist*

OVERGENERALIZATION

You make a broad, generalized conclusion based on a single incident. When is the last time you made too quick a conclusion based on a pilot change project? When a change initiative fails just slightly, do you jump on it immediately, declaring that the change will not work in your environment? You may be falling prey to the overgeneralization attitude.

LABELING

Instead of describing your error, you attach a negative label to yourself. How often do we label ourselves when we make an error? We say things like, "I'm so stupid." "I'll never amount to anything." "What a jerky thing to do. I am such an idiot." Ouch! We label our

> By attempting to avoid the responsibility for our own behavior, we are giving away our power to some other individual or organization. In this way, millions daily attempt to escape from freedom.
> M. Scott Peck

behavior, we label the organization, we label change, and then that's what we talk about. We need to realize that we become what we think about. Our thoughts become actions which develop into habits which build our character. Do you like what you are building?

> *"I am excited and challenged!! I believe the changes will benefit the consumer. The focus is more consumer-focused. We are finally viewing our services more holistically. My focus must stay on the goal — I cannot lose sight of what we are trying to accomplish. Change is the constant — we expect changes. What we are working towards — better service delivery — remains constant."*
>
> *Individual Support Facilitator*

CHANGING YOUR MIND TO POSITIVE SELF-TALK

Positive self-talk is a coping mechanism which can reduce stress by shifting you into a problem-solving mode. Here are some examples of positive and negative self-talk before, during, and after situations:

Before:

"*I am* handling this; I've handled similar change situations in the past."

"What specifically bothers me about this? Why is it a problem?"

"What's the worst thing that can happen? Would it really be that bad?"

During:

"*I am* taking one step at a time and am not jumping ahead."

"Getting upset will only make things worse; *I am* staying clear-headed."

"The only behavior I can control is my own. *I am* doing my job well until the change announcement is made."

After:

"*I am* keeping my mind focused on work and getting the job done."

"*I am* learning from this situation so the change will be easier."

"I was extremely upset about the proposed changes to my job, but I kept my emotions under control and spoke rationally."

What we need to do is to rationally analyze our negative self-talk statements and rewrite them to be positive and proactive. It's important to begin each statement with "I am ..." because positive self-talk only works when it is focused on the things we can control.

Let me give you two examples. Instead of thinking to yourself after a recent performance appraisal with your new boss, "Since I didn't receive perfect ratings in every area of my latest performance appraisal, I'm a failure in my job." Let's rewrite that statement to be ... "I am good at what I do as a (position). In my recent performance evaluation, I received almost all "4s" and "5s", so I plan to continue my current levels of performance in those areas. In the area of internal departmental communication, I received a "3," which is "average or meets standards." This is how I plan to bring my rating up to at least a "4" at my next evaluation . . ." You may also want to consider talking with your new boss by utilizing the skills discussed in Chapter 6.

> When we cling, often forever, to our old patterns of thinking and behaving, we fail to negotiate any crisis, to truly grow up, and to experience the joyful sense of rebirth that accompanies the successful transition into greater maturity.
>
> M. Scott Peck

Here's a second example. Instead of saying, "The presentation I gave at the department staff meeting last month did not come off as well as I would have liked, so I am convinced that my next presentation will also be a failure." You might try instead to say, "I am well prepared for my presentation at this week's department meeting, and I know that it will be well received."

Please note that the self-talk for the performance evaluation example came after the fact, while in the presentation example the statement came *before*. Both will work, depending on the situation.

> You need enough internal security to afford the risks of thinking abundantly and sharing power, knowledge, recognition, gain, and profit with other people.
> Stephen R. Covey

We must realize that we can be very susceptible to the negative influences of other people. However, we all have control over our beliefs and thoughts. Eleanor Roosevelt was right. No one can make us feel inferior, angry, frustrated, or resistant to change unless we allow ourselves to feel that way. We need to examine whether or not we want to BECOME what we say to ourselves. Although we often hear the comment, "you are what you eat," I think it is far more important to remember that "you are what you think."

AIM FOR A POSITIVE ATTITUDE

Here is a simple yet powerful technique for you to use each morning when you wake up. Focus your **AIM** on: (1) what you Appreciate, (2) your Intentions for the day, and (3) how will you Make a difference in the lives of others today.

APPRECIATE

Name three things you appreciate or are thankful for in the last twenty-four hours. Force yourself to come up with three new things every single day. Try not to repeat the same three things, such as: "I'm thankful for my family, my health, and that I have a job." Get creative. Here are some of mine: "I appreciate it when my house is clean." "I'm thankful for a tutor that helps my son Bryan keep on track with his writing." "I appreciate the cut on my hand because it reminds me of the fact that I have two hands that help me do a multitude of things." You might want to keep an AIM Journal for those days when you just can't think of anything. We take so much for granted. Just read the newspaper headlines and you should be able to come up with lots of things you are grateful that have not happened to you.

INTENTIONS

Each day, we need to focus on what we intend to do that day. Declare three things that you intend to do in the next twenty-four hours. Write your intentions down. Use post-it notes to remind yourself of your commitments. Here are some starter ideas:

- Give someone an encouraging word.
- Compliment your boss.
- Share a funny story with someone.
- Go the extra mile in your project.
- Make someone smile today.
- Give someone a hug.
- Listen with your full attention.

MAKE A DIFFERENCE

What three things will you do in the next twenty-four hours to make a difference in your life and in the lives of those around you? How will you change your self-talk to be more positive? Will you choose to wake up fifteen minutes earlier to get some meditation time in? Eat breakfast? Greet the people in your office with a big smile and greeting? Send your significant others off to work and/or school with a huge hug and kiss? Write a positive little note to slip into your family members' lunch bag? Open the door for someone today? Volunteer in your community or church? Give yourself a break when you make a mistake and make a mental note for how to be more proactive next time? Say thanks? Leave a generous tip?

"We have had an enormous amount of personnel changes and as a result I am exhausted and always wondering what will be next. For the most part I am forward thinking and I am excited about change. I am not resistant to change — rather I am tired of change physically, emotionally, and mentally."

Director of Leadership Programs

HALLWAY HELLOS

Did you know that people can tell a lot about you when they pass you in the hallways? One of my favorite things to do is to walk and greet people in the hallways of life. This is usually how it works . . . "Good morning (or afternoon). How are you?" Most people glumly say, "Fine. How are you?" I always enthusiastically reply, "Great!" They always turn around once I've passed them and say, "Boy, she must not work here."

If we want to feel great, we have to "fake it till we make it." Remember the mirroring technique? When you mirror someone, you actually begin to feel the same way they are feeling. You are experiencing empathy to the nth degree. Think about it. When we look down at the floor, we begin to feel depressed. That's because our focus is on OUR problems and OUR difficulties. It is tough to feel great about anything. But look at the difference it makes in how we feel when we look up and smile at other people.

Research indicates that a lot of physical sickness or a lack of "health in our bones" is due to worry, stress, and a lack of joy in our hearts. When it comes to saying positive things, I think that often we have to fake it until we make it. You have to say things to yourself that perhaps you don't initially

> A cheerful look brings joy to the heart, and good news gives health to the bones.
> Proverbs 15:30

believe. For example, I wasn't yet a national professional speaker when I first began saying that statement. I had to say it and believe it before it actually became true. You will have to do the same.

PERSONAL APPLICATION IDEAS:

 List the negative self-talk statements that you have about yourself, your workplace, and changes you are experiencing.

 Now write a positive self-talk statement to counter the negative thoughts you outlined in question one.

 Start an AIM Journal to record (1) what you Appreciate, (2) your Intentions for the day, and (3) how will you Make a difference in the lives of others today.

 Evaluate who your friends are. With whom did you go to lunch? Do you "whine and dine"? Do you come back to work with a great attitude or slumping shoulders? Pick and choose with whom you eat and what you discuss. Don't get into whining and dining with those people who can't make a difference in your organization's change.

ACTION PLAN
IT'S NOT WHETHER YOU WIN OR LOSE, IT'S THAT YOU'RE PLAYING THE GAME

"I made a complete job change. I can now see the plan come together, we can advocate for our clients and make the new planning system a true reality. Now when we see the glass half-full, we can assist with filling it up. It has opened our minds to new avenues."

Primary Service Coordinator

It takes time for us to see how the organizational change either worked or didn't work. Our job is to focus each and every day on what we can influence or control. To help with this, we need to design an Action Plan to move ourselves forward in the organizational change — for our own good as well as for the good of our organization.

Following is a list of seventy action items we can do to positively influence change. Each strategy includes a space for you to jot down notes about your progress and the results of your actions.

MY PERSONAL ACTION PLAN

1. What are my signals or warning signs that indicate I am in pain over a change situation? Identify how I cope with loss

and pain during change situations, i.e., my "cat" reactions. I know that the more quickly I can recognize my feelings of pain, the more quickly I will be able to identify where I am in the Cycle of Resistance. I am developing specific strategies to move myself forward in change.

Today's Date: _____

Progress Notes:_____

_____

_____

2. How has my organization communicated the change to its employees (memos, intranet, newsletter, etc.)? What sources of information do I have to keep abreast of these changes? I am constantly looking for ways to keep myself up-to-date with the changes in my organization and industry.

Today's Date: _____

Progress Notes:_____

_____

_____

3. I proactively forecast changes in my organization by determining ways to identify and anticipate industry trends.

Today's Date: _____

Progress Notes:_____

_____

_____

4. I position myself for success by developing new skills in anticipation of the potential changes in my organization. I have joined an industry association. I am a change agent.

Today's Date: _____

Progress Notes:_____

_____

_____

5. I refuse to fall prey to the "Most Valuable Player" syndrome when I feel my job security is threatened. I focus only on my own job performance and do not downplay a co-worker's job performance to build my advantage. I will stay professional despite the unknown factors.

    Today's Date: _____

    Progress Notes:_____

    _____

    _____

6. I count the personal costs of the organizational change I am going through. I am determining what decisions and choices I must make in order to move forward in my changes. I am minimizing the costs to me personally.

    Today's Date: _____

    Progress Notes:_____

    _____

    _____

7. I develop my personal boundaries at work. Examples: I will work only ___ hours of overtime. I will travel no more than ___ overnights per month. I am creating a career development plan in case my personal boundaries are overridden consistently by organizational demands. I will not let professional commitments ruin my personal life.

    > Only the wisest and stupidest of men never change.
    > Confucius

    Today's Date: _____

    Progress Notes:_____

    _____

    _____

8. I identified an objective, trustworthy person who can give
    me honest feedback on how I have been reacting through-
    out this organizational change. I ask for periodic feedback
    from him or her.

    Today's Date: _____

    Progress Notes:_____

    _____

    _____

9. I am managing my boss. I am observing the interactions my
    boss has with other people. I am specifically noting if the
    boss is interested in lots of details or just the bottom line. I
    identify whether she prefers competition over cooperation. I
    note what her pet peeves are. I understand when she is
    angry. I am dealing with my boss as she would like to be
    dealt with.

    Today's Date: _____

    Progress Notes:_____

    _____

    _____

10. In my next one-on-one meeting with my boss, I make a con-
    scious choice to mirror him. What did I learn about him by
    "acting" (mirroring) him? I make a mental note as to
    whether he is low-key or easily excitable. I watch to see
    whether he prefers thinking before speaking or if he quickly
    draws his conclusions. I consistently mirror my boss and
    develop a good rapport and trust level with him.

    Today's Date: _____

    Progress Notes:_____

    _____

    _____

11. I identify the information that would be important to a new leader in my organization. I determine in what format my boss would most appreciate this information. I am proactive about obtaining and providing this information to my boss as a way of partnering with him or her.

Today's Date: _____

Progress Notes:_____

_____

_____

12. I seek feedback on projects or assignments before a potential miscommunication can occur and mistakes become a crisis. If I am not clear about what my supervisor wants from me, I will ask questions.

Today's Date: _____

Progress Notes:_____

_____

_____

13. I ask my boss and others for positive feedback where none may be offered.

Today's Date: _____

Progress Notes:_____

_____

_____

14. I keep a "ME File" with examples of work I am especially proud of, letters of appreciation, and notes of congratulations I have received throughout the years. I review my "ME File" when I am feeling down and need an encouraging boost because of criticism from others.

> If you don't like something, change it. If you can't change it, change your attitude. Don't complain.
> Maya Angelou

Today's Date: _____

Progress Notes:_____

_____

_____

15. I listen carefully to my critic(s) to make sure I understand the criticism.

Today's Date: _____

Progress Notes:_____

_____

_____

16. Although I am coachable, I do not automatically assume my critic is right or wrong. I take the time to assess whether or not the criticism is valid before taking action. I ask questions to clarify the criticism or get specific examples of where I was wrong.

Today's Date: _____

Progress Notes:_____

_____

_____

17. I evaluate the source of criticism and whether it was offered constructively (gives me action to consider and is future-oriented), or destructively (used words such as "always, never, should") and is focused on the past.

Today's Date: _____

Progress Notes:_____

_____

_____

18. I do not passively accept criticism or become a silent victim. I am coachable.

Today's Date: _____

Progress Notes:_____

_____

_____

19. When I make a mistake, I do not overapologize or overcompensate. I freely admit my errors rather than trying to cover up.

Today's Date: _____

Progress Notes:_____

_____

_____

20. I don't make globally negative assessments about my character or ability based on one mistake, e.g., "I'm such a jerk! I'll never be any good at this." I give myself credit for past victories and accomplishments.

Today's Date: _____

Progress Notes:_____

_____

_____

21. I lower my emotional temperature and use positive self-talk when dealing with criticism, such as "I'm OK. I may have made a mistake, but learning from this error will increase my professionalism."

    Today's Date: _____

    Progress Notes:_____

    _____

    _____

22. I make a list of what/who I need to forgive. I note what I felt about what happened and what was done to me. I choose to forgive the person/organization. I will determine what method I will use — silence or reconciliation.

    Today's Date: _____

    Progress Notes:_____

    _____

    _____

23. I acknowledge my role in past forgiveness situation. I list what I can do to prevent the situation from happening in the future. I identify the lessons I have learned.

    Today's Date: _____

    Progress Notes:_____

    _____

    _____

24. I ascertain to whom I need to go and ask for forgiveness. I have thought through the difficult situations I have been avoiding and have taken action on them.

    Today's Date: _____

    Progress Notes:_____

    _____

    _____

25. I evaluate who my friends are. With whom do I go to lunch? Do I "whine and dine?" Do I come back to work with a great attitude or slumping shoulders? I pick and choose with whom I eat and what we will discuss. I will not allow myself to get into whining and dining with those people who can't make a difference in my organization's change.

> If we don't change, we don't grow. If we don't grow, we aren't really living.
>
> Gail Sheehy

Today's Date: _____

Progress Notes:_____

_____

_____

26. I only "whine with purpose" to those who impact and determine change in my organization. I use the DASS script and plan what I will say to them rather than reacting in anger or whining and dining with those who can't impact the change.

Today's Date: _____

Progress Notes:_____

_____

_____

27. In order to "let go" of old tasks and processes, I implement strategies to improve the organization's business processes. Bureaucracy Elimination: I identify the unnecessary administrative tasks, approvals, and paperwork that can be eliminated.

Today's Date: _____

Progress Notes:_____

_____

_____

28. Duplication Elimination: I name the identical activities that are performed in several places or at different points in the process.

Today's Date: _____

Progress Notes:_____

_____

_____

29. Simplification: I suggest ways that we could reduce the complexity of our department's processes or procedures. I list ways we could make our paperwork more uniform.

Today's Date: _____

Progress Notes:_____

_____

_____

30. Standardization: I recommend uniform ways of doing some of our department activities/processes/procedures/paperwork so that we all can do the activity the same way and save time.

Today's Date: _____

Progress Notes:_____

_____

_____

31. Automation and/or Mechanization: I am open to and look for ways to apply tools, technology, equipment, and computers to boring, routine activities to free me to do more creative activities.

Today's Date: _____

Progress Notes:_____

_____

_____

32. Communication: I locate the problems with the current means of communication within our department and make suggestions for how to improve. I discuss with my manager how I would like my manager to communicate to me. I share with my manager how would I like to communicate to him or her.

    Today's Date: _____

    Progress Notes:_____

    _____

    _____

33. Teamwork: I determine specific ways I can be more effective in my job and with my team. I suggest ways my managers can be more effective in their jobs and in promoting team-work, and I have discussed the ideas with them.

    Today's Date: _____

    Progress Notes:_____

    _____

    _____

34. I give input when none is asked.

    Today's Date: _____

    Progress Notes:_____

    _____

    _____

35. I encourage my co-workers when they are discouraged.

    Today's Date: _____

    Progress Notes:_____

    _____

    _____

36. I volunteer to serve on transition task forces.

Today's Date: _____

Progress Notes:_____

_____

_____

37. I keep my attitude positive.

Today's Date: _____

Progress Notes:_____

_____

_____

38. I help to improve department morale by encouraging cooperation and passing on information.

Today's Date: _____

Progress Notes:_____

_____

_____

39. I show kindness to others.

Today's Date: _____

Progress Notes:_____

_____

_____

40. I consistently get to work on time and am ready to work.

Today's Date: _____

Progress Notes:_____

_____

_____

41. I provide positive feedback to others.

Today's Date: _____

Progress Notes:_____

_____

_____

42. I improve my personal productivity and work habits.

Today's Date: _____

Progress Notes:_____

_____

_____

43. I implement the skills learned in this book (mirroring, whining with purpose, etc.).

Today's Date: _____

Progress Notes:_____

_____

_____

44. I enhance the quality of my work.

Today's Date: _____

Progress Notes:_____

_____

_____

45. I improve my communication skills (up, down, and with co-workers).

Today's Date: _____

Progress Notes:_____

_____

_____

46. I commit to my own personal safety.

    Today's Date: _____

    Progress Notes:_____

    _____

    _____

47. I develop and stick to a regular fitness routine.

    Today's Date: _____

    Progress Notes:_____

    _____

    _____

48. I determine how much sleep I require. I take control of my sleep habits.

    Today's Date: _____

    Progress Notes:_____

    _____

    _____

49. I use my VCR to tape my favorite late shows so I can watch them earlier the next day.

    Today's Date: _____

    Progress Notes:_____

    _____

    _____

50. I use a personalized browser to scan the Internet rather than surfing all night.

    Today's Date: _____

    Progress Notes:_____

    _____

    _____

51. I find the local weather information, sports scores, or other timely items on the World Wide Web instead of staying up for the late TV news.

Today's Date: _____

Progress Notes: _____

_____

_____

_____

_____

> The entirety of one's adult life is a series of personal choices, decisions. If we can accept this totally, then we become free people. To the extent that we do not accept this we will forever feel ourselves victims.
> M. Scott Peck

52. I get up fifteen minutes earlier than usual to meditate and to eat breakfast.

Today's Date: _____

Progress Notes:_____

_____

_____

53. I determine what foods I need to eliminate and add to my diet in order to lessen my stress response.

Today's Date: _____

Progress Notes:_____

_____

_____

54. I name three good friends who are outside of my family. I make a "date" now to spend time with them during the next month.

Today's Date: _____

Progress Notes:_____

_____

_____

55. I write a personal note or e-mail a friend I haven't spoken to in awhile.

Today's Date: _____

Progress Notes:_____

_____

_____

56. I schedule a "date" with my significant other so that she or he remains "significant."

Today's Date: _____

Progress Notes:_____

_____

_____

57. I develop my sense of humor by redefining how I react to things.

Today's Date: _____

Progress Notes:_____

_____

_____

58. I seek to recapture some of the joy and wonderment I experienced as a child.

Today's Date: _____

Progress Notes: _____

_____

I cannot say whether things will get better if we change; what I can say is they must change if they are to get better.
G.C. Lichtenberg

_____

_____

59. I take humor breaks.

    Today's Date: _____

    Progress Notes:_____

    _____

    _____

60. I strive to be people-oriented. I do a kind deed for someone each day.

    Today's Date: _____

    Progress Notes:_____

    _____

    _____

61. I share my humor with others.

    Today's Date: _____

    Progress Notes:_____

    _____

    _____

62. I build a laugh library.

    Today's Date: _____

    Progress Notes:_____

    _____

    _____

63. I look for humor behind words, associations, and situations.

    Today's Date: _____

    Progress Notes:_____

    _____

    _____

64. I list all the negative self-talk statements that I have about myself, my workplace, and changes I am experiencing. I write a positive self-talk statement to counter the negative thoughts I listed.

Today's Date: _____

Progress Notes:_____

_____

_____

65. I start an AIM Journal to record (1) what I Appreciate, (2) my Intentions for the day, and (3) how I Make a Difference in the lives of others today.

Today's Date: _____

Progress Notes:_____

_____

_____

66. When I am frustrated, I review my AIM Journal and am encouraged and uplifted.

Today's Date: _____

Progress Notes:_____

_____

_____

67. I let go of the things I do not control and make a graceful exit.

Today's Date: _____

Progress Notes:_____

_____

_____

68. I refuse to get sucked into the negative attitudes of others. I am a cheerleader in my organization.

Today's Date: _____

Progress Notes:_____

_____

_____

69. I take action on the things I can control and put on my game face.

Today's Date: _____

Progress Notes:_____

_____

_____

70. I decide that regardless of whether or not I have any control in my change situation, I am a change agent and not a change victim.

Today's Date: _____

Progress Notes:_____

_____

_____

When the British company downsized my division and me along with it, I had two choices: I could become a change agent or a victim of change. No one can force us to move forward with organizational changes or make us resistant to change. Only we can choose to become "change agents" or "change victims" — it is our choice. I chose to become The CHANGE AGENT and a professional speaker and author. My hope and prayer in writing this book is to help you determine why and how you can become a change agent in your situation. I'd love to hear from you about what works for you (see the free offer in the next section). I hope my book has taught you the following . . .

Change Agents are winners who are always part of the solution,
Victims are whiners who are always part of the problem.

Change Agents listen, get real, and tell the truth;
Victims fear the truth and tell people what they want to hear.

Change Agents value the pain of resistance and get to Yes;
Victims value Yes and ignore the pain of resistance.

Change Agents put on their Game Face and just do it!
Victims criticize from the sidelines and just hang on.

Change Agents say, "It's difficult, but it can be done."
Victims say, "It can be done, but it's too difficult."

FREE OFFER

For more information, to receive our free e-mail newsletter, or to order any of our products, please contact:

The CHANGE AGENT℠
1016 Woodglen Road
Westerville, Ohio 43081
Toll-free: 1-800-339-0973
Phone: 614-523-3633
Fax: 614-523-3515
E-mail: Patti@thechangeagent.com or Jim@thechangeagent.com
Website: http://www.thechangeagent.com

If you would like to receive our free e-mail newsletter filled with ideas on change, communication, and customer service, go to our website at http://www.thechangeagent.com and sign up.

If you have a great story or quote to share for possible inclusion in my e-mail newsletter, articles, or future books, please send or e-mail it to me. I'm very interested in real life stories on change and how change impacts customer service. Case Studies (great and poor examples) are particularly welcome.

We also have the following products and services described on our website or call us for more information on:

- Keynote speaking
- Full- or half-day on-site training programs customized for your specific organizational change issues
- *Giving and Receiving Feedback* book
- *Managing Upward: Strategies for Succeeding with Your Boss* book
- Audio and Video Cassette Learning Programs
- Personal telephone consultations with Patti
- Coaching Program for individuals
- "Key Ideas" laminated Card

- Quotoon Computer Screen Saver (a full-color set of all of the cartoons you enjoyed in this book)
- Framed and matted 11x14 full-color Quotoons (from the cartoons you enjoyed in this book)
- Quotoon Greeting Cards with envelopes
- "Not Secret" post-it notes

QUICK ORDER FORM

Fax Orders: (614) 523-3515. Send this form.

Telephone Orders: Toll-free call 1-800-339-0973; (614) 523-3633. Have your credit card ready.

E-mail Orders: Jim@thechangeagent.com

Postal Orders: Destination Publications, Jim Hathaway, 1016 Woodglen Road, Westerville, Ohio 43081-3236. USA.

Please send the following books or products. I understand that I may return any of them for a full refund — for any reason, no questions asked.

_____

_____

_____

Please send more FREE information on:
❏ Speaking/Seminars
❏ Coaching/Consulting
❏ Other books and products

Name:_____

Address:_____

City: _____State:____Zip: _____

Telephone: _____

E-mail Address: _____

Sales tax: Please add 5.75% for products shipped to Ohio addresses.

Shipping and Handling: $3 for the first book or product and $.75 for each additional product.

International: $9 for first book or product and $2 for each additional product (estimate).

Payment: ❏ Check ❏ Credit Card:

❏ Visa ❏ MasterCard ❏ American Express

Card number: _____

Name on card: _____Exp. Date: _____

Signature: _____